MATH-A-LOGIC

Written by Dianne Draze

Routledge
Taylor & Francis Group

NEW YORK AND LONDON

First published in 2010 by Prufrock Press Inc.

Published in 2021 by Routledge
605 Third Avenue, New York, NY 10017
2 Park Square, Milton Park, Abingdon, Oxon OX14 4RN

Routledge is an imprint of the Taylor & Francis Group, an informa business

Copyright © 2010 by Taylor & Francis Group

ISBN: 9781593631079 (pbk)

DOI: 10.4324/9781003236566

Contents

Information for the Instructor

Math and Logic

If you thought that math was all numbers, then you're in for a surprise. Numbers and the computational operations make up only a small part of the field of mathematics. More generally mathematics is a way of thinking and reasoning. It includes not only addition and subtraction, algebra and trigonometry, but also set theory and logic. It can be an analysis of the statement "All adults are tall" as well as the statement "2 + 10 = 12." The California Mathematics Framework says this about the role of logic in mathematical instruction:

The ability to reason logically is both a prerequisite for learning mathematics and a desired outcome of mathematics instruction. Mathematics provides an excellent context in which to make students aware of the logical structures they need to function successfully in any setting.

Logic is a field that began as a field of philosophy. The first attempt to define it as a discipline was made by Aristotle in 300 B.C. During the 19th century mathematical or symbolic logic was developed from the earlier logical system. This type of logic used symbols to express ideas. In fact, the main premise of Bertrand Russell's *Principia Mathematica* was that all mathematics was ultimately reducible to logic.

About This Book

Math-a-Logic combines math and logic and is designed to introduce young learners to the principles of logic as they are applied to mathematics. It does not delve deeply into the theories of philosophers and mathematicians who have advanced the study of logic or pursue the answer to the question "what is truth?". Instead it introduces several basic logical concepts and gives practice in the kind of logical thinking that has applications to real life. In almost all exercises, mathematics is the vehicle for presenting and practicing the logical concepts, thus giving students practice in mathematical concepts and computations while building thinking skills. The end result should be clearer thinking and enhanced problem-solving abilities.

There are eight different sections in this book. These sections are:

- **Patterns and Sequences** - In this first section students are asked to discover the patterns that exist in a set of numbers and then extend that pattern to produce the missing numbers.

- **Analogies** - Analogies are another form of looking for patterns and applying those patterns. In this case, students will be given two numbers and asked to discover the relationship between those two numbers and then apply the relationship to produce a second set of numbers with the same connection.

- **Deduction** - The problems in this section are presented as situations in which numerical information must be linked with people or things. The information is presented in the form of clues, and students must "read between the lines" or combine information from a couple of clues to solve the puzzle.

- **Inference** - There are several different kinds of problems in this section. In all these exercises, students will be using experimentation to arrive at the correct answer. While in a strict logical/mathematical sense this type of reasoning would be used to examine premises and then derive generalized assumptions based on these premises, the problems that are presented will give students an introduction to this type of experimental thinking.

- **Sets and Venn Diagrams** - Venn diagrams are used as visual representations of logical relationships. To add interest and to give students concrete examples, the problems use sets that are things and letters as well as numerals.

- **Propositions and Logical Notation** - In this section students are introduced to the concepts of logical notation, the transitive property, negation, truth values, and conditional statements. In order to aid students in grasping these concepts, many of the statements reflect real life rather than numerical relationships. In this section, as with the next one, students are still exercising reasoning that is applicable to mathematics even when they deal with problems that are filled with words rather than numbers.

- **Syllogisms** - This section presents one of the oldest of all logical problems. Students will be asked to analyze premises and conclusions to determine if the arguments are valid or not.

- **Logical Problem Solving** - This last section gives students problems that require a variety of problem-solving techniques as well as logical thinking to solve. Students should be encouraged to approach the problems with an open mind and try different approaches until they are able to solve each problem. You may wish to assign just one problem rather than all three problems on the page, as some of the problems could be quite challenging and time-consuming. As much as possible, students should be encouraged to explain the thinking that enabled them to solve the problem.

Introduction to Sequences

A **sequence** is a set of numbers, letters or objects. When the things in the sequence are arranged so that they follow a pattern, they are also called a **progression**. By looking at the relationships between the numbers, you can discover the pattern.

| *Examples* | 5, 7, 9, 11 | add 2 |
| | 10, 7, 4, 1 | subtract 3 |

Look at the following sequences. Decide what the next number should be. Write that number on the line.

1. 3,   7,   11,   15, _____

2. 4,   10,   16,   22, _____

3. 2,   5,   8,   11,   14, _____

4. 5,   20,   35,   50, _____

5. 9,   16,   23,   30, _____

6. 1/4,   1/6,   1/8,   1/10, _____

7. 21,   24,   27,   30, _____

8. 4,   9,   14,   19,   24, _____

9. 90,   85,   80,   75, _____

10. 19/20,   17/20,   15/20,   13/20, _____

11. 3/30,   4/35,   5/40,   6/45, _____

12. 2 1/2,   3 2/3,   4 3/4,   5 4/5, _____

13. 11,   20,   29,   38,   47, _____

14. 26,   24,   22,   20, _____

15. □□ □□ □□ □□□ _____

© Taylor & Francis Group · *MATH-A-LOGIC*   DOI: 10.4324/9781003236566-1

Changing Sequence Patterns

Sometimes sequences have changing patterns.

Examples   2, 3, 5, 6, 8   add 1, add 2

              16, 14, 15, 13, 14   subtract 2, add 1

Look at the following sequences. Decide what the next number should be. Write that number on the line.

1. 2,   5,   4,   7,   6,   _____

2. 10,   15,   17,   22,   24,   29,   _____

3. 25,   22,   19,   16,   _____

4. 100,   80,   85,   65,   70,   _____

5. 25,   30,   40,   45,   55,   _____

6. 17,   13,   19,   15,   21,   _____

7. 33,   31,   28,   26,   23,   _____

8. 14,   16,   13,   15,   12,   _____

9. 2 2/4,   4 4/8,   6 6/12,   8 8/16,   _____

10. 1/10,   2/10,   3/10,   4/10,   5/10,   _____

11. 1.2,   3.7,   6.2,   8.7,   _____

12. .75,   .55,   .60,   .40,   .45,   _____

13. 13,   17,   22,   28,   35,   _____

14. .5,   1.5,   3.0,   5.0,   7.5,   _____

15. 1,   3,   6,   10,   15,   _____

Geometric Progressions

Sometimes sequences are formed by multiplying or dividing numbers or by using some combination of multiplication and division.

Examples	*1,*	*10,*	*100,*	*1,000*	*multiply by 10*
	100,	*20,*	*4,*	*4/5*	*divide by 5*
	10,	*20,*	*5,*	*10, 2.5*	*multiply by 2, divide by 4*

Look at the following sequences. Decide what the next number should be. Write that number on the line.

1. 2,   4,   8,   16,   _____

2. 1,   3,   9,   27,   _____

3. 1/4,   1/8,   1/16,   1/32,   _____

4. 10,   1,   .1,   .01,   _____

5. 5,   10,   20,   40,   _____

6. 2/3,   4/9,   8/27,   16/81,   _____

7. 7.0707,   70.707,   707.07,   7070.7,   _____

8. 1/10,   2/50,   4/250,   8/1250,   _____

9. 500,   25,   1.25,   .0625,   _____

10. 1,000,   300,   90,   27,   _____

11. 5,   10,   30,   60,   180,   _____

12. 100,   200,   50,   100,   25,   _____

13. 10,   30,   60,   80,   110,   _____

14. 1,   1/3,   1/6,   1/18,   1/36,   _____

15. 4,   12,   24,   72,   144,   _____

Interrupted Sequences

Some of the sequences in this lesson include interrupted sequences. These sequences either have a constant element that repeats or have two sequences that are mixed together.

| *Examples* | 1, 1, 2, 1, 3, 1, 4, 1, 5 | *the number 1 is placed between the counting numbers* |
| | 2, 3, 4, 6, 6, 9, 8, 12 | *multiples of 2 alternate with multiples of 3* |

Add the next two elements to each progression.

1. 7, 2, 9, 3, 11, 4, 13, 5, _____, _____

2. 33, 31, 28, 24, _____, _____

3. 1, 2, 3, 5, 8, _____, _____

4. 15, 10, 20, 15, 30, 25, _____, _____

5. 2, 3, 6, 3, 18, 3, 54, 3, _____, _____

6. 2, 1/2, 3, 2/3, 4, 3/4, _____, _____

7. 3, 1/3, 9, 3/9, 27, 9/27, _____, _____

8. 1/3, 1/7, 1/11, 1/15, _____, _____

9. 100, 10, 20, 2, 4, .4, _____, _____

10. 2, 2, 4, 6, 10, 16, _____, _____

11. 2, 2, 4, 2, 8, 2, 16, 2, _____, _____

12. 1, 9, 2, 18, 3, 27, 4, 36, _____, _____

13. 5, 10, 12, 24, 26, 52, _____, _____

14. 1,000, 100, 101, 10.1, 11.1, _____, _____

15. 1, 2, 2, 2, 4, 2, 8, 2, 16, _____, _____

Sequences with Sixes

All the following sequences begin with the number six, but they are different types of sequences. Study the numbers in each progression to discover the pattern. Add the next two elements of each progression.

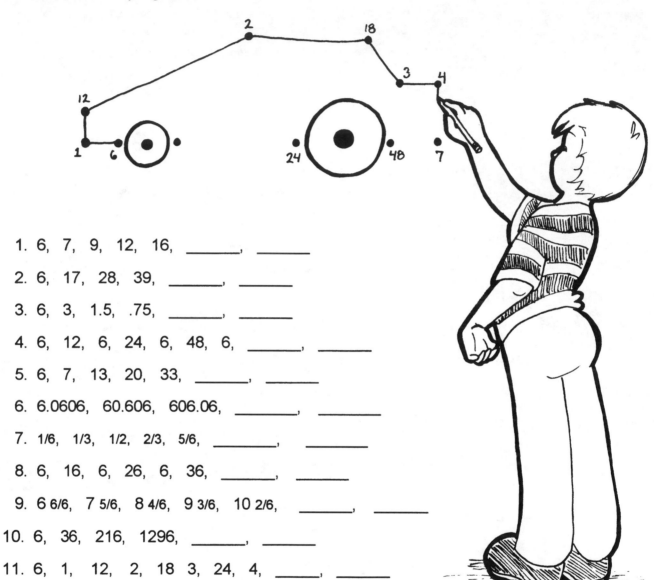

1. 6, 7, 9, 12, 16, _____, _____

2. 6, 17, 28, 39, _____, _____

3. 6, 3, 1.5, .75, _____, _____

4. 6, 12, 6, 24, 6, 48, 6, _____, _____

5. 6, 7, 13, 20, 33, _____, _____

6. 6.0606, 60.606, 606.06, _____, _____

7. 1/6, 1/3, 1/2, 2/3, 5/6, _____, _____

8. 6, 16, 6, 26, 6, 36, _____, _____

9. 6 6/6, 7 5/6, 8 4/6, 9 3/6, 10 2/6, _____, _____

10. 6, 36, 216, 1296, _____, _____

11. 6, 1, 12, 2, 18 3, 24, 4, _____, _____

12. 6, 12, 18, 24, 30, _____, _____

13. 6, 12, 14, 28, 30, 60, _____, _____

14. 6, 16, 36, 66, 106, _____, _____

15. 6, 8, 11, 15, 20, _____, _____

16. 6, 3, 7, 3, 8, 3, 9, _____, _____

Sequence Review

The numbers in the following sequences are related in a variety of ways. Study the sequence and discover the pattern. Then add the missing number or numbers to each progression.

1. .978, 9.78, 97.8, _____, _____

2. 2, 6, 12, 20, 30, 42, _____, _____

3. 2500, 250, 25, _____, _____

4. 123, 234, 345, _____, _____

5. 2, 4, 7, 11, 16, _____, _____

6. 1, 3, 2, 5, 3, 7, 4, _____, _____

7. 1/2, 1/3, 1/4, 1/3, 1/8, _____, _____

8. 4/13, 6/15, 8/17, 10/19, _____, _____

9. 9001.96, 900.196, 90.0196, 9.00196, _____, _____ .

10. 1, 3, 2, 4, 3, 5, 4, _____, _____

11. 2, 7, 5, 10, 8, _____, _____

12. 4, 9, 16, 25, _____, _____

13. .5, .30, .10, .30, .15, .30, _____, _____

14. 1/2, 1/3, 2, 1/4, 1/5, 2, _____, _____

15. 5/6, 7/9, 9/12, 11/15, _____, _____

16. 2, 3, 3, 3, 4, 3, 5, _____, _____

Problem Solving with Patterns

Find a pattern that will help you solve the following problems.

1. Jessie is painting cubes that are stacked one on top of the other. He paints only the sides and top (not the bottom) of each cube. How many faces does he paint for 1 cube ? 2 cubes? 3 cubes? 10 cubes?

2. An inch worm crawling up the side of a hole climbs up 100 centimeters the first hour, 95 centimeters the second hour, 90 centimeters the third hour, and so forth. How many centimeters in all will it have traveled at the end of 12 hours?

3. How many dots will be in the 4th triangle? How many in the 10th triangle?

Problem Solving with Patterns

Find a pattern that will help you solve the following problems.

1. The Brown family always orders a 2-topping pizza. How many different combinations do they have to choose from if there are 3 toppings on the menu? 4 toppings? 15 toppings?

2. If 11 x 11 = 121 and 111 x 111 = 12,321, what will 111,111 x 111,111 be? (Try to figure this out without actually multiplying the numbers).

3. Paul is on a diet. When he started the diet he weighed 85 kilograms. The first month he lost 7 kilograms. The second month he gained 5 kilograms. The third month he lost 6 kilograms, and the fourth month he gained 4 kilograms. At this rate, how much will he weigh after 10 months?

Problem Solving with Patterns

Find the pattern that will help you solve these problems.

1. Look at this array of numbers.

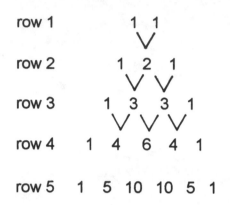

row 1 | | | | 1 | 1 | | | |
row 2 | | | 1 | 2 | 1 | | |
row 3 | | 1 | 3 | 3 | 1 | |
row 4 | 1 | 4 | 6 | 4 | 1 |
row 5 | 1 | 5 | 10 | 10 | 5 | 1 |

What will be the first five elements of the 11th row of this array?

2. The sum of the angles of a triangle is 180°.
The sum of the angles of a quadrilateral is 360°.
The sum of the angles of a pentagon is 540°.
The sum of the angles of a hexagon is 720°.
Devise a formula for finding the sum
of the angles of any regular polygon.
What is the sum of the angles of a
dodecagon?

3. The Girl's Club does a one-dollar gift
exchange at Christmas each year.
Each girl buys a one-dollar gift for
every other member of the club. How
much money would be spent on gifts
by all the members of the club
together if there were 3 members? 5
members? 20 members?

Problem Solving with Patterns

Find the pattern that will help you solve these problems.

1. At the end of summer, Daphne divides her day lilies, each plant producing 2 new plants. If she started with one plant 5 years ago, how many plants will she have when she divides the plants at the end of the 5th summer?

2. When the queen counts her jewels, she finds she has 10 pearls for each diamond, 5 rubies and 6 sapphires for each diamond, and 3 emeralds for every 2 sapphires. How many jewels does she have all together if she has 1 diamond? 3 diamonds? 100 diamonds?

3. This chart shows Jake's savings. If he continues at this rate, how much money will he have at the end of 12 weeks?

Jake's Savings	
week	money saved
1	1.00
2	2.50
3	3.50
4	5.00
5	6.00

Introduction to Analogies

An **analogy** is a comparison between two sets of things. A relationship is set up between the first pair in the analogy and the same relationship must exist between the second pair.

Examples   5 is to 6 as 14 is to 15

☐ is to ■ as ◯ is to ●

Analogies can also be written using **:** to mean "is to" and **::** to mean "as." So you can write analogies in the following way.

10 : 20 :: 44 : 88 which means **10 is to 20 as 44 is to 88**

In analogies involving numbers, you will be trying to determine what mathematical operation (or combination of operations) has been used for the first two things and applying that relationship to the second pair. Here are examples of analogies using various operations.

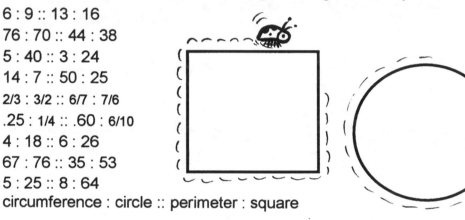

addition	6 : 9 :: 13 : 16
subtraction	76 : 70 :: 44 : 38
multiplication	5 : 40 :: 3 : 24
division	14 : 7 :: 50 : 25
inverse	2/3 : 3/2 :: 6/7 : 7/6
equivalents	.25 : 1/4 :: .60 : 6/10
combination	4 : 18 :: 6 : 26
reserving digits	67 : 76 :: 35 : 53
square	5 : 25 :: 8 : 64
vocabulary	circumference : circle :: perimeter : square

Tell what mathematical operation has been used for each of the following analogies. Write the correct letter on the line in front of the analogy.

1. _____ 5 : 25 :: 7 : 49   a. inverse

2. _____ 4 : 17 :: 17 : 30   b. square

3. _____ 80 : 40 :: 12 : 6   c. vocabulary

4. _____ 15 : 10 :: 24 : 19   d. addition

5. _____ .25 : 25/100 :: .8 : 8/10   e. combination

6. _____ circumference : circle :: perimeter : rectangle   f. equivalents

7. _____ 2 : 22 :: 5 : 52   g. subtraction

8. _____ 1/2 : 2 :: 5/6 :: 1 1/5   h. division

          © Taylor & Francis Group · *MATH-A-LOGIC*   DOI: 10.4324/9781003236566-2

Easy Analogies

Solve these analogies by looking at the relationship between the first two numbers and then choosing the number that completes that relationship in the second part of the analogy.

1. 4 : 5 :: 6 : _____
5
9
7
4

2. 4 : 40 :: 9 : ___
1/9
49
10
90

3. 6 : 3/6 :: 10 : ___
10 5/10
10 3/6
10/5
5/10

4. 2 3 4 : 4 3 2 :: 1 6 7 : ___
7 6 1
1 7 6
6 7 1
3 6 7

5. 7 : 17 :: 32 : ___
33
42
23
232

6. 2 : 5 :: 6 : ___
10
9
12
3

7. 25 : 5 :: 64 : ___
46
16
8
45

8. 10 : 100 :: 13 : ___
130
93
1300
163

9. 4 : 16 :: 9 : ___
19
22
81
35

10. 3 : 9 :: 4 : ___
9
12
18
16

11. 7 : 50 :: 11 : ___
55
78
150
121

12. 42 : 3 :: 70 : ___
5
7
10
14

Visual Analogies

These analogies involve geometric shapes. Look for the relationship between the first two shapes. Then choose the answer that relates to the second pair in the same way.

1. △ : △ :: ___
   a. ▽ : △
   b. ☐ : ☐
   c. ☐ : ▭

2. ● : ○ :: ___
   a. ● : ●
   b. ■ : ☐
   c. ☐ : ■

3. ☐ : ■ :: ___
   a. ■ : ☐
   b. ⬭ : ⬮
   c. ○ : ●

4. ▽ : △ :: ___
   a. ⌒ : ⌣
   b. ▭ : ▯
   c. ● : ◑

5. ○ : ⊘ :: ___
   a. ☐ : ⊞
   b. ☐ : ▭
   c. ○ : ◖

6. ⊟ : ⊟⊟ :: ___
   a. ☐ : ☐☐☐
   b. ● : ◓
   c. ● : ◑

7. ◍○○ : ○○◍ :: ___
   a. ○◍● : ◍●○
   b. ◧ : ◨
   c. ☐ : ⊟

8. △ : ▲ :: ___
   a. ☐ : ■
   b. ■ : ■
   c. ● : ○

9. △ : △△ :: ___
   a. ○ : ⚬⚬⚬⚬
   b. ☐ : ⊞
   c. ☐ : ⊞

All Star Analogies

Solve these analogies by looking at the relationship between the first two numbers and then choosing the number that completes that relationship in the second part of the analogy.

1. 7 : 6/7 :: 14 : ___

14/13
13/14
14 13/14
13

2. 2/3 : 4/9 :: 5/12 : ___

7/12
10/25
10/144
25/144

3. 6 : 3 :: 100 : ___

25
50
96
94

4. 15 : 7 :: 23 : ___

15
31
16
32

5. 5/13 : 10/13 :: 4/50 : ___

8/50
8/100
9/55
9/13

6. 12 : 13 :: IX : ___

IXX
IV
XI
X

7. 123 : 6 :: 567 : ___

8
12
18
765

8. 20 : 5 :: 56 : ___

7
14
8
5

9. 169 : 13 :: 36 : ___

9
6
13
63

10. 10 : 23 :: 6 : ___

20
12
9
15

11. 7 : 14 :: 12 : ___

24
18
6
21

12. 628 : 826 :: 248 : ___

421
124
842
824

Sailing Through Analogies

Solve these analogies by looking at the relationship between the first two numbers and then choosing the number that completes that relationship in the second part of the analogy.

1. 1 2 3 : 4 5 6 :: 4 5 6 : ___

6 5 4

6 7 8

7 8 9

6 8 10

2. 10 9 8 : 9 8 7 :: 5 4 3 : ___

3 4 2

4 3 2

4 5 6

7 6 5

3. 5¢ : 50¢ :: 10¢ : ___

65¢

$1.00

25¢

55¢

4. 9 : 19 :: 65 : ___

75

85

55

615

5. 5 : 26 :: 7 : ___

49

29

50

35

6. .25 : 1/4 :: .125 : ___

1/8

1/2

1/6

.50

7. 5 : 24 :: 24 : ___

48

43

19

5

8. 1/2 : 1/4 :: .50 : ___

1.00

.25

25/50

.52

9. ___ : 8 :: 56 : 7

15

78

64

71

10. ___ : .75 :: .73 : .23

.25

1.00

.50

1.25

11. ___ : 11 :: 81 : 9

91

98

11/9

121

12. 2/5 : ___ :: 3/4 : .75

.2

.40

.52

.25

Analogy Roundup

Solve these analogies by looking at the relationship between the first two numbers and then choosing the number that completes that relationship in the second part of the analogy.

1. 2 : 3 :: 100 : ___
    100 2/3
    200
    101
    99

2. 67 : 76 :: 59 : ___
    57
    95
    60
    5/9

3. 27 : 9 :: 99 : ___
    33
    11
    9
    101

4. 16 : 4 :: 100 : ___
    10,000
    20
    90
    10

5. 20 : 5 :: 48 : ___
    4
    12
    1/4
    38

6. 2/3 : 1/3 :: 50 : ___
    1/5
    1/50
    5
    25

7. 63 : 79 :: 15 : ___
    24
    36
    31
    30

8. 1/2 : 3/2 :: 6.7 : ___
    7.7
    6/7
    7/6
    5.7

9. 99 : 77 :: 53 : ___
    55
    31
    33
    42

10. 6.3 : 2.1 :: 4.2 : ___
    2.1
    2.4
    1.2
    1.4

11. 3/4 : 9/4 :: 3.1 : ___
    1/3
    3.9
    9.3
    9.1

12. 6 : 78 :: 21 : ___
    210
    94
    273
    252

Math Scores

Five students (Josh, Becca, Romeo, Ian and Julia) compared their scores on a math test. Their math scores were 100, 98, 96, 80, and 78. Use the clues to match each person with their score.

Clues

1. Josh scored higher than Julia and Ian.
2. Romeo's score was 20 more than Ian's but less than Becca's.

Fast Animals

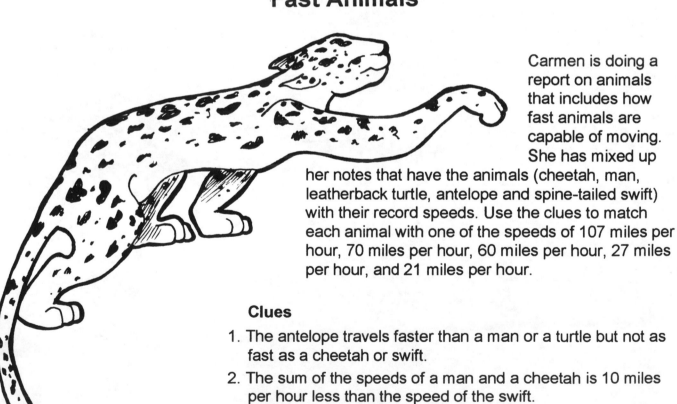

Carmen is doing a report on animals that includes how fast animals are capable of moving. She has mixed up her notes that have the animals (cheetah, man, leatherback turtle, antelope and spine-tailed swift) with their record speeds. Use the clues to match each animal with one of the speeds of 107 miles per hour, 70 miles per hour, 60 miles per hour, 27 miles per hour, and 21 miles per hour.

Clues

1. The antelope travels faster than a man or a turtle but not as fast as a cheetah or swift.
2. The sum of the speeds of a man and a cheetah is 10 miles per hour less than the speed of the swift.
3. A man can run faster than a turtle can swim but cannot run as fast as an antelope.

© Taylor & Francis Group · *MATH-A-LOGIC*

DOI: 10.4324/9781003236566-3

First Day of School

It's the first day of school and the three children in the Smith family are looking for their new rooms. They are in different grades (1st, 4th, and 6th) in school, and their classes are held in different rooms. Use the clues to match each child with their grade and room number (room 2, room 5, room 17).

Clues

1. Haley and the first grader do not have to walk upstairs to the rooms numbered 11 through 20.
2. Jonathan is older than Tanya and his room number is higher than hers.
3. Jonathan and the person in room 5 and the 6th grader walk home together after school.
4. The first grader has a room number that is greater than the 6th grader.

Raffle Winners

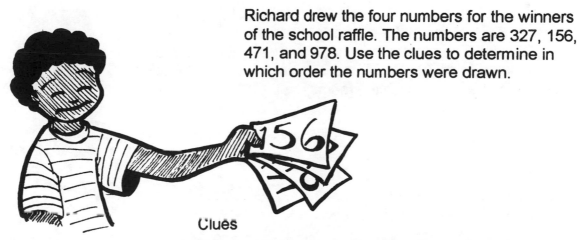

Richard drew the four numbers for the winners of the school raffle. The numbers are 327, 156, 471, and 978. Use the clues to determine in which order the numbers were drawn.

Clues

1. The sum of the second and fourth numbers is one third the sum of the first and third numbers.
2. The third number is 24 more than the sum of the other three numbers.
3. The second number is less than half of the fourth number.

Family Ages

The ages of the members of the Mendez family (Mr. Mendez, Mrs. Mendez, Amy, Alex, Andy and Anton) are 4, 5, 10, 15, 33 and 34 years. Match each person in the family with their correct age.

Clues

1. Mrs. Mendez's age is the sum of her children's ages.
2. Anton's and Alex's ages when added together equal Andy's age.
3. Andy's age is three times Anton's age.

Team Scores

Four teams (Troy Tigers, Chicago Cubs, Lincoln Lions and Evanston Eagles) are in the play-offs for the state basketball championship. Their top scores that won them a place in the championship were 79, 84, 94 and 99 points. Use the clues to match up the scores with the teams.

Clues

1. The sum of the Cubs' and Lions' scores equals the sum of the Tigers' and Eagles'.
2. The Eagles scored 5 more than the Cubs and 10 less than the Tigers.

Jim's Garden

Jim has a garden that is divided into six sections. Read the clues and refer to the drawing to discover what is planted in each section.

Clues

1. The number of pepper plants equals the sum of the squash plants and the tomato plants.
2. The marigolds border the tomatoes.
3. The squash are planted in the section between sunflowers and the tomatoes.
4. Jim has weeded the sections containing sweet peas and peppers but not the cabbage between these two sections.
5. Jim has twice as many tomatoes as sunflowers and twice as many sweet peas as tomatoes.

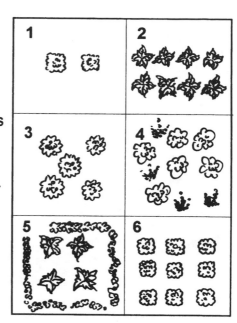

Cake Lottery

Five friends (Catherine, Charles, Dee, Matt, and Stacy) drew numbers (5, 7, 18, 23, and 25) from a hat to determine who would win the prize at the school carnival's cake lottery. Use the clues to find out who drew which number.

Clues

1. Charles' number is greater than Stacy's but less than Dee's.
2. Dee's number is divisible by Matt's number.
3. Catherine's number plus Stacy's number equals Dee's number.
4. Matt's number plus Stacy's number equals Charles' number.

Animal Temperatures

Edward's report on animals includes a section on body temperature. He is reporting on the spiny anteater, rain frog, spiny lizard, icefish, peewee bird and goat. He has found body temperatures of 112°, 104°, 98°, 80°, 74° and 30° F. Use the clues to match each animal with its body temperature.

Clues

1. The frog's body temperature is greater than the anteater and the icefish but less than the lizard.

2. The goat's temperature is greater than the lizard but less than the peewee's.

3. The icefish's temperature is less than half the anteater's.

Space Jumper

Sarah is doing a report on planets that includes information on each planet's gravity and on the number of moons for each planet. She is calculating how far a person would be able to jump on each planet. She finds that a 1 meter jump on Earth would result in heights of 2.68, 2.60, 1.11, .85, .82 and .41 meters on Jupiter, Neptune, Mars, Saturn, Mercury and Venus. She has also found that the planets have 19, 16, 2, 2, 0 and 0 moons. Use the clues to help you match up each planet with the height a person could jump on that planet.

Clues

1. Venus, the other planet with zero moons, and Mars all have jumps higher than on Earth.

2. The planet with the lowest jump has three less moons than the planet with a .85 meter jump but 14 moons more than the planet with a jump that is twice as high.

3. Saturn has a higher jump and more moons than Jupiter or Neptune but a lower jump than Mars and the two planets with no moons.

4. Neptune and the planet with the 2.60 meter jump have one moon more than Earth and two more than Mercury and the planet with a 1.11 meter jump.

5. A jump on Neptune would be twice as high as a jump on Jupiter.

Two-Digit Scavenger Hunt

Use the clues to help you discover the secret number.

1. It's a two-digit number.
   The first digit is even.
   The sum of the two digits is 11.
   The second digit is 3 more than the first digit.
   The number is _____ _____.

2. It's a two-digit number.
   Both of the digits are multiples of 3.
   The second digit is three more than the first digit.
   The number is less than 90 but greater than 40.
   The number is _____ _____.

3. It's a two-digit number.
   The second digit is three times the first digit.
   Both digits are even numbers.
   The number is _____ _____.

4. It's a two-digit number.
   It is an even number.
   The difference between the digits is 5.
   The number is greater than 40 and less than 70.
   The number is _____ _____.

5. It's a two-digit number.
   It is odd.
   The sum of the digits is 10.
   It is greater than 20 but less than 50.
   The number is _____ _____.

Three-Digit Scavenger Hunt

Use the clues to help you discover the secret number.

1. It is a three-digit number.

   All the digits are odd.

   The second digit is 2 more than the first digit.

   The third digit is 4 more than the second digit.

   The number is less than 300.

   The number is ____ ____ ____.

2. It is a three-digit number.

   The first and third digits are the same.

   It is odd.

   The second digit is less than the first and third digits.

   The sum of the digits is 15.

   The number is ____ ____ ____.

3. It is a three-digit number.

   The sum of the last two digits equals the first digit.

   The first and the third digits are odd.

   The first digit is 1 more than the second.

   The sum of all three digits is 10.

   The number is ____ ____ ____.

4. It is a three-digit number.

   The digits are consecutive numbers.

   The number is odd.

   It is greater than 400.

   5 is not one of the digits.

   The number is ____ ____ ____.

Mystery Pairs

Find the numbers to make these math statements true. In each problem the same shape stands for the same number in both number sentences.

1. ○ + □ = 14
    ○ - □ = 4

6. □ + ○ = 6
    ○ × □ = 8

11. ○ + □ = 9
    □ ÷ ○ = 2

2. □ + ○ = 35
    ○ - □ = 15

7. □ + ○ = 18
    ○ × □ = 45

12. ○ × □ = 14
    □ - ○ = 5

3. ○ + □ = 14
    □ × ○ = 48

8. ○ - □ = 9
    □ × ○ = 36

4. ○ - □ = 6
    ○ × □ = 40

9. ○ - □ = 5
    ○ × □ = 150

5. □ + ○ = 42
    ○ - □ = 4

10. □ - ○ = 16
    ○ + □ = 18

More Mystery Pairs

Find the numbers that will make these math statements true. In each problem the same shape stands for the same number in both of the number sentences.

1. $\bigcirc + \square = 31$
   $\bigcirc - \square = 1$

2. $\bigcirc + \square = 19$
   $\square \times \bigcirc = 34$

3. $\square + \bigcirc = 8$
   $\bigcirc \times \square = 15$

4. $\bigcirc + \square = 41$
   $\square - \bigcirc = 33$

5. $\bigcirc + \square = 24$
   $\bigcirc \div \square = 7$

6. $\bigcirc + \square = 64$
   $\square \div \bigcirc = 15$

7. $\bigcirc + \square = 17$
   $\square \times \bigcirc = 42$

8. $\bigcirc + \square = 66$
   $\square - \bigcirc = 38$

9. $\bigcirc + \square = 20$
   $\bigcirc \div \square = 4$

10. $\bigcirc - \square = 36$
    $\bigcirc \div \square = 5$

11. $\bigcirc + \square = 55$
    $\bigcirc - \square = 9$

12. $\bigcirc - \square = 6$
    $\bigcirc \times \square = 55$

Challenger

Find the missing numbers in each problem. In each
problem, the same shape stands for the same number.

7 ☐

1. -2 ☐

☐ ◯

☐ 3

3. $-2\ 9$

◯ ☐

☐ ☐

6. $+$ ◯ 7

6 ◯

1 ◇ ☐

9. $+$ ☐ 1 8

◯ ◯ 1

◇ 2

2. $+$ ◇ 0

☐ ☐

4 9 ☐

4. $-$ ☐ ◯

4 ◯ 5

☐ ◇

7. $+3$ ◇

◇ ☐

☐ ◯ 7

10. $+$ ◇ 9

◯ ☐ ◯

---

5. $+$ ◇ ◇

1 ◇ 3

9 ☐

8. -1 ◯

☐ ◯

☐ ◇

11. $+$ ◇ 6

1 3 ☐

Brain Stretcher

Find the missing numbers in each problem. In each problem, the same shape stands for the same number.

1.
```
    ○ ○ ○
  x _____ □
  1 ○  ○ 2
```

2.
```
    1 □
  x ___ □
    7 □
```

3.
```
    ◇  8
  x ___ ◇
    5  6
```

4.
```
    8 □
  x ___ 5
  □ 2 0
```

5.
```
    7 7
  x ___ □
  2 □ 1
```

6.
```
  1 □  3
  x ___ ○
  ○ 9 □
```

7.
```
       □ 1
  □ ) 3 □ □
```

8.
```
       8 2
  □ ) 5 □ 4
```

9.
```
         1 □ 1
  1 □ ) 1 □ 1 □
```

10.
```
        4 0 1
  1 □ ) □ 4 1 □
```

11.
```
       □ 9
  9 ) □ 6 1
```

Number Arrays

1. Arrange the numbers 10, 15, 20, 25 and 30 in the squares so that the sums vertically and horizontally are 60.

2. Arrange the numbers 6, 7, 8, 9 and 10 in the squares so that the sums vertically and horizontally are 24.

3. Arrange the numbers 11, 13, 15, 17 and 19 in the squares so that the sums vertically and horizontally are 45.

4. Arrange the numbers 1, 3, 5, 7 and 9 so that the sums vertically and horizontally are 17.

5. Arrange the numbers 6, 8, 10, 12 and 14 so that the sums vertically and horizontally are 30.

6. Arrange the numbers 5, 6, 7, 8 and 9 so that the sums vertically and horizontally are 21.

Number Shuffle

1. Arrange the numbers 1, 2, 3, 4, 5, 6, 7, 8 and 9 so the sums vertically and horizontally are 25.

2. Arrange the numbers 3, 6, 9, 12, 15, 18, 21, 24 and 27 so the sums vertically and horizontally are 75.

3. Arrange the numbers 2, 4, 6, 8 and 10 so that the sums vertically and horizontally are 18.

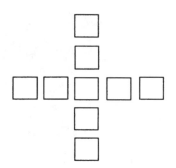

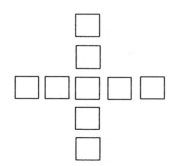

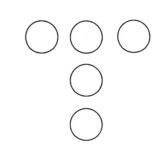

4. Arrange the numbers 10, 11, 12, 13, 14, 15, 16, 17 and 18 so the sums vertically and horizontally are 70.

5. Arrange the numbers 5, 6, 7, 8, 9, 10, 11, 12 and 13 so the sums vertically and horizontally are 45.

6. Arrange the numbers 4, 8, 12, 16, 20, 24, 28, 32 and 36 so that the sums vertically is horizontally are 100.

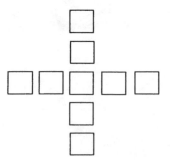

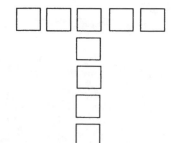

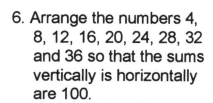

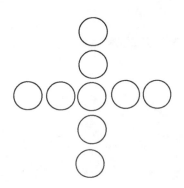

Magic Squares

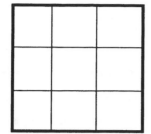

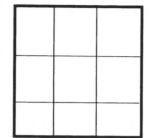

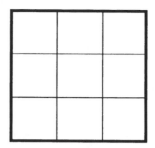

1. Arrange the numbers 1, 2, 3, 4, 5, 6, 7, 8 and 9 in the squares so that the sums of all the rows, columns and diagonals are 15.

3. Arrange the numbers 3, 6, 9, 12, 15, 18, 21, 24 and 27 in the squares so that the sums of all the rows, columns and diagonals are 45.

5. Arrange the numbers 4, 8, 12, 16, 20, 24, 28, 32 and 36 in the squares so that the sums of all the rows, columns and diagonals are 60.

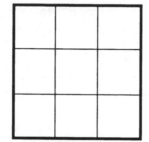

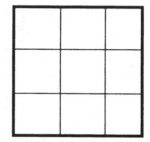

2. Arrange the numbers 2, 4, 6, 8, 10, 12, 14, 16 and 18 in the squares so that the sums of all the rows, columns and diagonals are 30.

4. Arrange the numbers 4, 5, 6, 7, 8, 9, 10 and 11 in the squares so that the sums of all the rows, columns and diagonals are 24.

6. Arrange the numbers 5, 10, 15, 20, 25, 30, 35, 40 and 45 in the squares so that the sums of all the rows, columns and diagonals are 75.

Magic Square Mastery

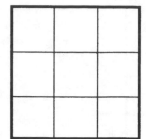

1. Arrange the numbers 20, 22, 24, 26, 28, 30, 32, 34 and 36 in the squares so that the sums of all the rows, columns and diagonals are 84.

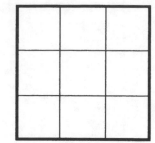

4. Arrange the numbers 10, 11, 12, 13, 14, 15, 16, 17 and 18 in the squares so that the sums of all the rows, columns and diagonals are 42.

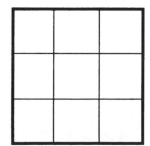

2. Arrange the numbers 3, 4, 5, 6, 7, 8, 9, 10 and 11 in the squares so that the sums of all the rows, columns and diagonals are 21.

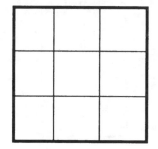

5. Arrange the numbers 6, 7, 8, 9, 10, 11, 12, 13 and 14 in the squares so that the sums of all the rows, columns and diagonals are 30.

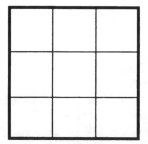

3. Arrange the numbers 25, 27, 29, 31, 33, 35, 37, 39 and 41 in the squares so that the sums of all the rows, columns and diagonals are 99.

6. Arrange the numbers 2, 6, 10, 14, 18, 22, 26, 30 and 34 in the squares so that the sums of all the rows, columns and diagonals are 54.

Find the Rule

State the rule and add the missing numbers for each problem.

1. Rule _____

10	5
6	3
20	
18	

2. Rule _____

6	0
40	34
92	
81	

3. Rule _____

3/2	2/3
4/3	3/4
10/23	
19/5	

4. Rule _____

6	6 1/2
15 1/2	16
23 1/2	24
1/2	

5. Rule _____

606	60.6
40	4
	18
50.8	

6. Rule _____

4	45
7	75
11	
26	

7. Rule _____

30	15
17	2
45	
93	

8. Rule _____

30	10
9	3
42	
93	

9. Rule _____

25	5
81	9
36	
144	

10. Rule _____

2	103
99	200
63	
44	

11. Rule _____

5	30
6	42
9	90
13	

12. Rule _____

50	10
5	1
15	
95	

Rule Roundup

State the rule and fill in the missing
numbers for each problem.

1. Rule _____

2	4
7	14
10	
16	

2. Rule _____

15	5
33	11
300	
6	

3. Rule _____

5	1/5
10	1/10
7	
32	

4. Rule _____

4	7
9	12
16	
22	

5. Rule _____

14	4
23	13
50	
46	

6. Rule _____

49	7
16	4
100	
25	

7. Rule _____

2/3	4/3
6/20	12/20
1/5	
4/9	

8. Rule _____

4	15
10	33
7	24
21	

9. Rule _____

7	6/7
13	12/13
27	
	3/4

10. Rule _____

2	4
9	81
8	
14	

11. Rule _____

13	25
7	19
19	
40	

12. Rule _____

90	79
15	4
33	
28	

Introduction to Sets

A **set** is a collection or group of objects. It can be a group of numbers, people, or things. The objects in the set are called the **elements** of the set. We use brackets **{ }** to enclose the elements of the set.

Examples {1, 2, 3, 4}

{chickens, cows, ducks, sheep}

A set with no elements in it is called the **empty** or **null set**. It is shown as a set with empty brackets **{ }** and the symbol is **Ø**.

A set can be named by using a capital letter.

Example

A = {2, 4, 6, 8}

F = {apple, sandwich, milk, cookie}

Match the sets on the left with the descriptions on the right.

1. ___ {1, 3, 5, 7, 9}

2. ___ {vanilla, chocolate, strawberry}

3. ___ {fork, knife, spoon}

4. ___ {5, 10, 15, 20, 25}

5. ___ {1, 2, 3, 4, 6, 12}

6. ___ {x, y, z}

7. ___ { }

8. ___ {100}

9. ___ {February}

a. empty set

b. last three letters of the alphabet

c. first five multiple of 5

d. first five odd numbers

e. most common flavors of ice cream

f. utensils used for eating

g. divisors of 12.

h. months with 28 days

g. whole numbers greater than 99 but less than 101

Write the elements of these sets.

10. colors of the rainbow _____

11. multiples of 3 between 1 and 20 _____

12. first five even numbers _____

13. friends whose names begin with J _____

Finite and Infinite Sets

Sets may have a limited or **finite** number of elements, like the set of the first three letters of the alphabet {a, b, c}.

Sets may also have an unlimited or **infinite** number of elements like the set of whole numbers {0, 1, 2, 3, 4, . . .}. We use dots at the end of the initial listing of the elements to indicate that the list goes on and on without ending.

If a set is finite but we don't want to write all the elements, we can write the first few elements, write three dots and then write the last element. The set whose elements are the letters of the alphabet could be written as {a, b, c, d,. . . z}.

Write the elements of these sets.

1. The set of counting numbers less than 10 _____

2. The set of even numbers between 1 and 100 _____

3. The set of letters in your first name _____

4. The set of months starting with the letter M _____

5. The set of numbers less than 100 that are divisible by 10 _____

6. The set of fractions greater than 0 that have 5 as a denominator _____

7. The set of odd whole numbers _____

8. The set of teachers who teach the grade you are in _____

9. The set of principals in your school _____

10. The set of divisors of 6_____

11. The set of words that can be made using the letters S, T, P, O _____

_____

12. The set of whole numbers that are greater than 10 but less and 200 _____

_____

Subsets

A set is said to be a **subset** of another set if all its elements are contained in the other set.

Example

If A = {1, 2, 3} and B = {1, 2, 3, 4, 5}, then set A is a subset of B because every element of A is contained in B.

➤ We can write **A ⊂ B**, which says *"A is contained in B."*

➤ We can also write **B ⊃ A**, which says *"B contains A."*

Example

C = {100, 102, 104, 106} and D = {100, 101, 102, ...} then D ⊃ C or C ⊂ D

➤ Also we can say that if A ⊂ B and B ⊂ A, then A = B.

Example

E = {c, a, t} and F = {t, c, a}, then E ⊂ F and F ⊂ E and E = F

Match these sets and their subsets.

1. ___ {1, 2, 3, 4, 5}   A = {teachers}

2. ___ {2, 4, 6, 8}   B = {1, 3, 5}

3. ___ {5, 10, 15 ... 100}   C = {people in your neighborhood}

4. ___ {school days}   D = {Sunday, Saturday}

5. ___ {weekend days}   E = {car, truck, boat}

6. ___ {people living in your town}   F = {8}

7. ___ {n, k, o, s, t}   G = {rose, lily}

8. ___ {boys, girls, teachers}   H = {k, n, o, t, s}

9. ___ {means of transportation}   I = {Tuesday, Wednesday}

10. ___ {rose, lily, snapdragon, daisy}   J = {horses}

11. ___ {animals}   K = {90, 95, 100}

12. Which sets are equal? _____

Writing Subsets

Remember that a set is a subset of another set if all its members are also members of the larger set. If we write A ⊂ B or B ⊃ A, it means that all the members of set A are contained in set B or A is a subset of B.

Example

If A = {1, 3, 5, 7, 9} and B = {1, 2, 3, 4, 5, 6, 7, 8, 9}, then A ⊂ B.

If C = {food} and D = {cookies, cakes, pies}, then C ⊃ D

If E = {birds in the aviary} and F = {animals in the zoo}, then E ⊂ F.

For each of the following sets, write a smaller set that is a subset.

1. {a, b, c, d, e, f} _____

2. {prime numbers} _____

3. {even numbers} _____

4. {people in your classroom} _____

5. {programs on television} _____

6. {100, 101, 102, ...150} _____

7. {24, 27, 30, 33, 36, 39, 42} _____

8. {red, orange, yellow, green, blue, violet} _____

9. {hammer, saw, level, nails} _____

10. {1, 2, 3, 5, 8, 13, 21, 34...} _____

11. {girls with blond hair} _____

12. {socks, shoes, pants, shirt, coat, gloves, hat} _____

13. {trout, bass, catfish, salmon, shark, halibut} _____

Adding Sets

When two sets are added together, the resulting set contains all the elements of both sets. The sum of the sets is called the **union**. The symbol is ∪.

Examples

A = {0, 1, 2} and B = {3, 4, 5}   A ∪ B = {0, 1, 2, 3, 4, 5}

C = {1, 3, 5} and D = {5, 7, 9}   C ∪ D = {1, 3, 5, 7, 9}

Write the sum or union of these sets.

1. A = {cat, dog, fish}
   B = {turtle}

   A ∪ B = _____

2. A = {2, 4, 6, 8}
   B = {1, 3, 5, 7}

   A ∪ B = _____

3. A = {girls in room 4}
   B = {boys in room 4}

   A ∪ B = _____

4. A – {1, 3, 5, 7   }
   B = {2, 4, 6, 8...}

   A ∪ B = _____

5. A = {1, 2, 3, 4, 6, 12}
   B = {1, 2, 4, 8}

   A ∪ B = _____

6. A = {1, 2, 3, 4, 5, 6}
   B = {1, a, 2, b, 3, c, 4, d, 5, e, 6}

   A ∪ B = _____

7. A = {p, a, i, n, t}
   B = {b, r, u, s, h}

   A ∪ B= _____

8. A = {s, p, r, i, t, e}
   B = {c, o, k, e}

   A ∪ b = _____

9. A = {m, o, n, d, a, y}
   B = {t, u, e, s, d, a, y}

   A ∪ B = _____

10. A = {0, 1, 2}
    B = {1/2, 1, 1 1/2}

    A ∪ B = _____

Set Intersection

Another function of sets is intersection. The **intersection** of two sets is all those elements that are in both sets (all the elements that they have in common). The symbol for intersection is ∩.

Examples

A = {1, 2, 3, 4} and B = {3, 4, 5, 6}   A ∩ B = {3, 4}

C = {c, a, t} and D = {d, o, g}   C ∩ D = { } or the empty set

E = {m, i, l, k} and F = {j, u, i, c, e}   E ∩ F = { i }

Find the intersection of these sets.

1. A = {5, 10, 15, 20, 25}
   B = {10, 20, 30}

   A ∩ B = _____

2. A = {2, 4, 8, 16, 32}
   B = {2, 4, 6, 8, 10, 12, 16}

   A ∩ B = _____

3. A = {1, 2, 3, 6}
   B = {1, 2, 3, 4, 6, 12}

   A ∩ B = _____

4. A = {h, e, a, l, t, h, y}
   B = {s, i, c, k, l, y}

   A ∩ B = _____

5. A = {b, o, y, s}
   B = {g, i, r, l, s}

   A ∩ B = _____

6. A = {h, o, l, i, d, a, y}
   B = {c, h, r, i, s, t, m, a, s}

   A ∩ B = _____

7. A = {s, p, r, i, t, e}
   B = {c, o, k, e}

   A ∩B = _____

8. A = {m, o, n, d, a, y}
   B = {t, u, e, s, d, a, y}

   A ∩ B = _____

9. A = {f, i, s, h}
   B = {f, r, i, e, s}

   A ∩ B = _____

Set Summary

The **intersection** (∩) of two sets is the elements that are in both sets. The **union** (∪) of the two sets is all the elements that are in one set or the other set. If two sets have no members in common, the intersection is the **empty set** and the sets are said to be **disjoint**.

Example

A = {c, a, t} and B = {f, i, s, h}

A ∪ B = {c, a, t, f, i, s, h}

A ∩ B = { }

For each of the two sets below, write the members in the union and the intersection.

1. A = {cat, dog, fish, bird}
   B = {fish, frog, lizard}

   A ∪ B = _____

   A ∩ B = _____

2. C = {pie, cake}
   D = {peas, carrots}

   A ∪ B = _____

   A ∩ B = _____

3. E = {January, February}
   F = {December, January, February}

   A ∪ B = _____

   A ∩ B = _____

4. G = {h, o, m, e, l, y}
   H = {h, i, d, e, o, u, s}

   A ∪ B = _____

   A ∩ B = _____

5. I = {t, i, g, e, r}
   J = {l, i, o, n}

   A ∪ B = _____

   A ∩ B = _____

6. K = {2, 4, 6, 8, 10, 12}
   L = {4, 8, 12, 16, 20}

   A ∪ B = _____

   A ∩ B = _____

7. M = {girls in the 4th grade}
   N = {boys in the 4th grade}

   A ∪ B = _____

   A ∩ B = _____

8. O = {o, r, a, n, g, e}
   P = {v, i, o, l, e, t}

   A ∪ B = _____

   A ∩ B = _____

Working with Three Sets

The same rules for intersecting and forming the union of two sets can be applied to more than two sets. The intersection of three sets is the elements that appear in all three sets. The union of these three sets would be the elements that belong to any of the three sets.

$A = \{1, 2, 3\}$ $B = \{2, 3, 4, 5\}$ $C = \{3, 6, 9\}$.

$(A \cap B) \cap C = \{2, 3\} \cap \{3, 6, 9\} = \{3\}$

$(A \cup B) \cup C = \{1, 2, 3, 4, 5\} \cup \{3, 6, 9\} = \{1, 2, 3, 4, 5, 6, 9\}$

If you formed the intersection of A and B and then the union of that intersection, this is what you would have:

$(A \cap B) \cup C = \{2, 3\} \cup \{3, 6, 9\} = \{2, 3, 6, 9\}$

Find the intersection and union of these sets.

1. A = {p, e, a, r}
   B = {o, r, a, n, g, e}
   C = {g, r, a, p, e}

   $(A \cup B) \cup C =$ _____

   $(A \cap B) \cap C =$ _____

   $(A \cap B) \cup C =$ _____

3. G = {g, e, r, m, a, n, y}
   H = {h, u, n, g, a, r, y}
   I = {i, t, a, l, y}

   $(G \cap H) \cap I =$ _____

   $(G \cup H) \cup I =$ _____

   $(G \cap H) \cup I =$ _____

2. D = {2, 4, 6, 8, 10}
   E = {1, 2, 3, 4, 5, 6}
   F = {4, 8, 12}

   $(D \cup E) \cup F =$ _____

   $(D \cap E) \cup F =$ _____

   $D \cup (E \cap F) =$ _____

4. J = {1, 2, 3, 4, 6, 12}
   K = {1, 2, 3, 6, 9, 18}
   L = {1, 2, 5, 10}

   $(J \cup K) \cup L =$ _____

   $(J \cap K) \cap L =$ _____

   $J \cup (K \cap L) =$ _____

Introduction to Venn Diagrams

One way to picture sets and subsets is to draw a diagram of them. These diagrams are called Venn diagrams, named after a mathematician named Venn. Circles are used to show the sets. Three types of diagrams are possible.

➤ This shows two sets that have no common elements.

If A = {1, 3, 5, 7} and B = {2, 4, 6, 8}, this is what we would draw.

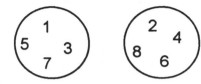

➤ This shows two sets with some common elements. These common elements are in the intersecting area.

If A = {1, 3, 5, 7} and B = {5, 7, 9, 11}, this is what we would draw.

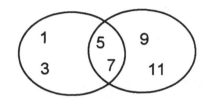

➤ This shows a set with its subset. Every element of the smaller set is an element of the larger set.

If A = {1, 2, 3, 4, 5, 6, 7} and B = {2, 4, 6}, this is what we would draw.

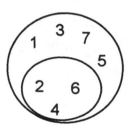

Draw a line between these sets and the Venn diagram that shows how they are related.

1. A = {boys}
   B = {girls}

a.

2. A = {things with fur}
   B = {things that live underground}

b.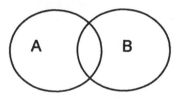

3. A = {animals}
   B = {cats}

c.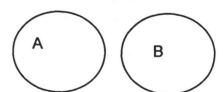

Put Them in Their Place

Look at these Venn diagrams and tell what set each thing would fall in.

1. a girl who does not skateboard ____
2. a girl who does skateboard ____
3. a boy who does skateboard ____
4. a boy who does not skateboard ____

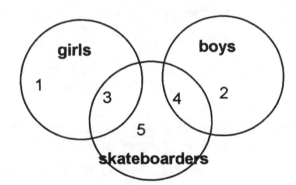

5. cat ____   10. kangaroo ____
6. horse ____   11. rabbit ____
7. frog ____   12. grasshopper ____
8. bear ____   13. elephant ____
9. giraffe ____

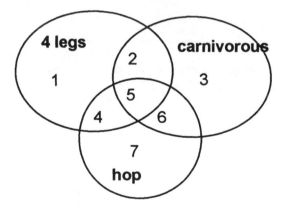

14. a person who only surfs ____
15. a person who hikes and bikes ____
16. a person who hikes and surfs ____
17. a person who hikes, bikes and surfs ____

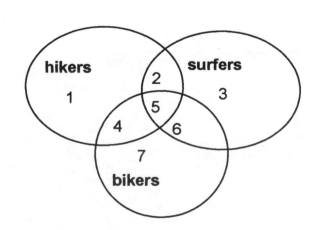

Drawing Venn Diagrams

Draw and label Venn diagrams for the intersection of these sets.

1. A = {10, 20, 30, 40, 50}
   B = {5, 15, 25, 35, 45}

2. A = {5, 10, 15, 20, 25}
   B = {10, 15, 20}

3. A = {school days}
   B = {Saturday, Sunday}

4. A = {people in our class}
   B = {boys in our class}

5. A = {12, 9, 6, 3, 1}
   B = {1, 2, 3, 6}

6. A = {chocolate, strawberry}
   B = {chocolate, vanilla}

Set Sketch

Draw and label Venn diagrams to show the intersection of the following sets.

1. A = {10, 20, 30, 40, 50}
   B = {5, 10, 15, 20, 25, 30}

2. C = {things that swim}
   D = {fish}

3. E = {males}
   F = {children}

4. G = {purple things}
   H = {flowers}

5. K = {mammals}
   L = {birds}
   M = {fish}

6. N = {blue things}
   O = {jeans}
   P = {clothes}

Sets Solo Flight

Follow the instructions in each problem to create your own Venn diagrams.

1. Take a survey to find out what kind of cars the families of the people in your class drive (domestically-made or foreign-made). Record the information in the Venn diagram.

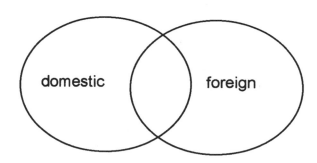

2. Find out how many people in your class are wearing the colors red, white or blue today. Record the information in the Venn diagram.

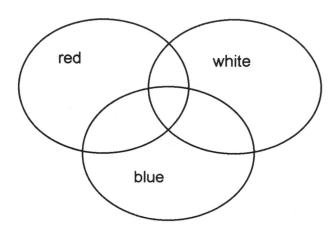

3. Choose three movies that are currently playing at the theaters or three books that are frequently read by people your age. Take a survey to find out how many people have seen each of the movies or read the books. Label the Venn diagram and record your data.

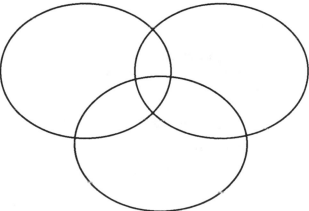

Solving Problems with Diagrams

Venn diagrams can be used to solve complex problems. You must first draw and label the sets that are used in the problem. Then copy the information from the problem into the appropriate places on the diagram. Then use the diagram to answer the questions.

1. In the annual Run/Jump-a-thon participants earned money by running, jumping rope or both. Thirty (30) students in the 5th grade took part in the event.

   10 people ran and jumped rope

   12 people only ran

   2 people were timers and did not run or jump

   How many people only jumped rope?_____

   If each of the runners had pledges of $5.00 and the jump ropers had pledges of $8.00 each, how much money did the class earn?_____

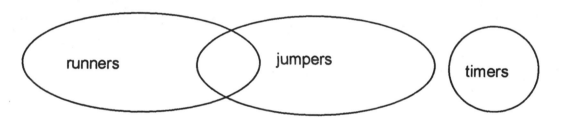

2. Twenty people were at a birthday party. Two did not stay for dessert. Of the people who stayed, 3 people ate cake only. Five people ate ice cream only.

   How many people ate both cake and ice cream?_____

   How many ate ice cream and/or cake?_____

   How many pieces of cake were served?_____

   How many servings of ice cream were needed?_____

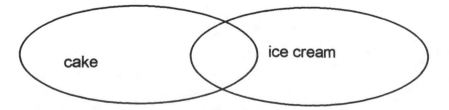

© Taylor & Francis Group • *MATH-A-LOGIC*

Mastering Set Problems

Draw your own Venn diagrams and then use them to solve these problems.

1. Mr. Hershey is taking a survey of his neighborhood to find out what kind of pets each family owns. He has the following information.
   1 family owns a cat, a dog and a bird.
   8 families own only cats.
   2 families own only birds.
   10 family own only dogs.
   4 own both a cat and a dog.
   2 own a bird and a dog.
   6 families own no pets.
   1 family owns a cat and a bird

   How many families own cats? _____

   How many families own dogs? _____

   How many families own birds? _____

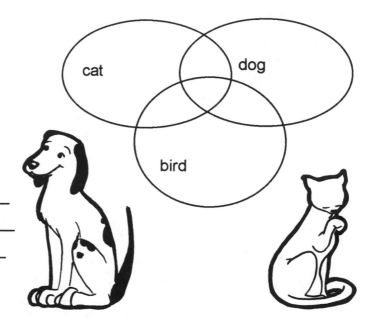

2. Students at Fairhaven School can choose from three electives — art, computers and photography. They can take either one or two classes.
   12 take both art and computers.
   10 take both computers and photography.
   12 take both art and photography.
   4 take only art.
   9 take only computers.
   3 take only photography.

   How many people are in the art class?_____

   How many people are in the computer class?_____

   How many people are in the photography class?_____

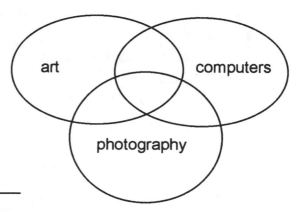

Untangling Set Problems

Draw Venn diagrams to help you solve these problems.

1. The Garden Club sent out a survey of its members to find out what kinds of plants the members could donate for the annual plant sale. These are the results of the survey:

   10 vegetables only
   4 herbs only
   15 flowers only
   2 flowers, herbs, and vegetables
   9 flowers and vegetables
   2 vegetables and herbs
   6 herbs and flowers

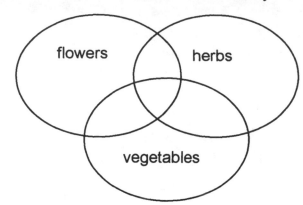

   How many will donate flowers? _____

   How many will donate herbs? _____

   How many will donate vegetables? _____

2. The principal of Westmont School was making a list of people who played in school sports during the year for the awards assembly. This is what she found.

   5 people played baseball and football.
   7 people played baseball and soccer.
   9 people played football and soccer.
   3 people played all three sports.
   39 played baseball and/or football.
   10 played football only.
   38 played soccer and/or football.

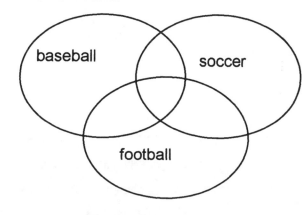

   How many played only baseball?_____

   How many played only soccer?_____

   How many players play in one or more sports during the year?_____

Introduction to Logical Notation

A **proposition** is a statement. It can be true or false.

"Ice is a form of water" is true.

"Ice is water in its gaseous state" is false.

"Two is an even number" is true.

"The sum of two odd numbers is an odd number" is false.

In logic we use special notation to show propositions so we do not have to write the entire statement. We use a letter or two letters to stand for a proportion.

R can stand for *"It is raining."*

BU can stand for *"Bring your umbrella."*

Propositions can be combined to form compound propositions using the words "and," "or" and "if...then." The symbol → stand for "if..then." This is called the **conditional proposition.**

GT and JS could stand for the sentence *"George is tall and Josh is short."*

GT or JS could stand for the sentence *"George is tall or Josh is short."*

R → BU could stand for the sentence *"If it is raining, then bring your umbrella."*

Match these propositions with their logical notation.

1. ____ It is hot and it is windy.

2. ____ You can go swimming.

3. ____ If it's hot, then you can go swimming.

4. __ The number is a multiple of ten.

5. ____ If the number ends in zero, then It is a multiple of 10.

6. ____ It is freezing and there is precipitation.

7. ____ If it is freezing and there is precipitation, then it will snow.

8. ____ A number is even or a number is odd.

9. ____ If a number is odd, then it is not divisible by 2.

10. ____ It is an insect or it is a spider.

a. MT

b. E or O

c. H → GS

d. F and P

e. O → ND

f. H and W

g. I or S

h. F and P → S

i. GS

j. EZ → MT

Review of Logical Notation

Here is a review of logical notation.

➢ A capital letter (or a combination of letters) can stand for an event or a simple thought.

   SM = *You spill your milk.*   **DL** = *The dog will lick it up.*

➢ → stands for "if...then" or "implies"

   SM → DL = *If you spill your milk, then the dog will lick it up.*

➢ AND statements and OR statements can be represented using capital letters for each of the separate thoughts.

   T = *Tanya is tall.*

   S = *Sarah is short.*

   T and S = *Tanya is tall and Sarah is short.*

   T or S = *Tanya is tall or Sarah is short.*

Match each statement with its logical notation.

1. ___ The figure is a quadrilateral.   a. Q

2. ___ If the figure is a quadrilateral, then it has four sides.   b. GR

3. ___ The angle is less than 90°.   c. A

4. ___ If the angle is less than 90°, then it is an acute angle.   d. TS

5. ___ The movie has a good rating.   e. GR → WS

6. ___ If the movie has a good rating, then I will see it.   f. Q → F

7. ___ Today is Saturday.   g. TS → S

8. ___ If today is Saturday, then I will go shopping.   h. A → AA

Write the following statements using logical notation. Use the letters in parenthesis.

9. The number is prime and it is odd. (N, P, O) _____

10. If the figure is a pentagon, then it has five sides. (F, F, P, S) _____

11. If you eat your vegetables, then you will be healthy. (E, H, Y, V) _____

Transitive Property

As you have already learned, one relation that may exist between propositions is one of implication, when one proposition implies another.

> ➤ The **transitive property** says that if proposition 1 implies proposition 2 and proposition 2 implies proposition 3, then proposition 1 implies proposition 3.
>
> *If P1 → P2 and P2 → P3, then P1 → P3.*

SS = The sun shines.

W = It will be warm.

SS → W = If the sun shines, then it will be warm.

If we had a third statement that said *"We will go swimming,"* we could write :

W → WS = If it is warm, then we will go swimming.

If SS → W and W → WS then SS → WS.

Write these statement as symbols.

1. If Bob comes (BC), then Jill will come too (JT). _____

2. If you keep pouring (YP), then the cup will overflow (CO). _____

3. If the cup overflows (CO), then it will make a mess (MM). _____

4. If you don't water your plant (WP), then it will die (D). _____

5. If you make a point (MP), then the crowd will cheer (CC). _____

6. If water is put in the freezer (WT), then it will turn solid (TS). _____

7. If a number is divisible by 20 (TW), then it is divisible by 10 (TE). _____

8. If a number is divisible by 10 (TE), then it is divisible by 5 (F). _____

9. Use the transitive property on problems 2, 3, 7, and 8 to write two new statements of implication and their symbols.

_____

_____

Negation

➤ ~ is a symbol that stands for negation. ~ says *"it is false that"* or *"not."* The **negation** of a statement has the opposite truth value. So if a proposition P is true, ~P is false.

JS = Julie is smart.

~JS = Julie is not smart.

~JS = It is false that Julie is smart.

➤ The negation of a negation is the original statement.

~D = It is not a daisy.

~~D = D = It is a daisy.

➤ To negate an AND statement, negate each part and change the "and" to "or."

H and R = It is hot and it is raining.

~(H and R) = ~H or ~R = It is not hot or it is not raining.

➤ To negate an OR statement, negate each part and change the "or" to " and."

NE or NO = The number is even or the number is odd.

~(NE or NO) = ~NE and ~NO = The number is not even and the number is not odd.

For each statement write its negation and then write the symbol for the negated statement.

1. The triangle has three sides. (TS) _____

2. It is not raining. (~R) _____

3. A square is a quadrilateral. (SQ) _____

4. The sum is even or the sum is odd. (SE or SO) _____

5. Mother can go and Father cannot go. (MG and ~FG) _____

_____

6. The cat is cute and the dog is dirty. (CC and DD) _____

_____

7. It is raining or it is not snowing (R or ~S) _____

Truth of Propositions

Like propositions, compound propositions and the negation of propositions also can be either true or false. The following rules for the truth of the propositions applies.

➢ **OR statements** are **true** if either proposition is true.

➢ **AND statements** are **true** only if both propositions are true.

➢ **NEGATION** has the **opposite truth value** of the proposition.

R = A rose is a flower. - True

Y = A rose is a vegetable. - False

R or Y is true because one of the statements (R) is true.

R and Y is false because only one of the propositions is true; not both of them.

~ R is false because R is true and the negation always has the opposite truth value.

Tell the truth of the following statements.

1. T = Triangles have three sides.
   S = Squares have four equal sides.

   a) T _____

   b) S _____

   c) T and S _____

   d) T or S _____

   e) ~T _____

2. P = The Pacific is larger than the Atlantic.
   O = The Arctic Ocean is located in the southern hemisphere.

   a) P _____

   b) O _____

   c) P and O _____

   d) P or O _____

   e) ~P _____

3. L = Lions bark.
   D = Ducks quack.

   a) L _____

   b) D _____

   c) L and D _____

   d) L or D _____

   e) ~D _____

4. P = Two is a prime number.
   E = Two is an even number.

   a) P _____

   b) E _____

   c) P and E _____

   d) P or E _____

   e) ~P or E _____

Practice with Truth Values

Tell whether the statement is true or false. Then write the negation and the symbol for the negation.

_____ 1. A triangle has three angles. (TA)

_____

_____ 2. B is a better grade than D. (BB)

_____

_____ 3. The product of two even numbers is not an even number. (~PE)

_____

_____ 4. The sun is a star or the sun is a planet. (SS or SP)

_____

_____ 5. Cats can fly and birds can swim. (CF and BS)

_____

_____ 6. Twelve is even and forty-three is odd. (TE and FO)

_____

_____ 7. A rectangle is a quadrilateral. (RQ)

_____

_____ 8. The hypotenuse is the longest side of a right triangle. (HL)

_____

_____ 9. Twelve has six factors and twelve is even. (SF and E)

_____

Truth Values of Conditional Statements

In order to determine if an if-then statement is true of not, we have to look at each individual part of the statement. The rule is that the statement is false only when the "if " part is true and the "then" part is false. If P and Q are two parts of an if-then statement, a table for determining truth would look like this:

P	Q	P → Q
T	F	F
T	T	T
F	F	T
F	T	T

Judge the truth value of each statement and the entire conditional statement. Write true or false on the lines following the logical notation for each statement.

1. If water is a liquid, then steam is a gas.

   WL _____   SG _____   WL → SG _____

2. If twenty is a multiple of ten, then twenty is even.

   MT _____   E _____   MT → E _____

3. If rain is purple, then snow is mauve.

   RP _____   SM _____   RP → SM _____

4. If two is a factor of six, then two is a factor of 12.

   FS _____   FT _____   FS → FT _____

5. If frogs are mammals, then frogs lay eggs.

   FM _____   LE _____   FM → LE _____

6. If Mercury is the planet closest to the sun, then Saturn is the most distant planot.

   MC _____   SD _____   MC → SD _____

7. If squares are rectangles, then squares are quadrilaterals.

   SR _____   SQ _____   SR → SQ _____

8. If France is a country in Europe, then France is adjacent to Norway.

   FE _____   FN _____   FE → FN _____

Review of Truth Values

The following is a list of the rules for truth values that you have learned so far.

➢ ~A has the opposite truth value of A.

➢ (A and B) is true only when A is true and B is true.

➢ (A or B) is false only when A is false and B is false.

➢ A → B is false only when A is true and B is false.

➢ To determine the truth value of a conditional statement that includes an AND statement or an OR statement, determine the truth of the AND or OR statement separately and then determine the truth of the whole if-then statement.

Examples

D = Dogs bark. (true)

C = Cats bark. (false)

A = Dogs and cats are animals. (true)

D and C = Dogs bark and cats bark. (false because both propositions are not true)

D or C = Dogs bark or cats bark. (true because one proposition is true)

(D and C) → A = If dogs bark and cats bark, then dogs and cats are animals (true because the "if" part is false, and the "then" part is true)

(D or C) → A = If dogs bark or cats bark, then dogs and cats are animals. (true because the "if" part and the "then" part are both true)

Use the following truth values for these four propositions to determine the truth values for the combinations of the statements.

     A - true   B - true   C - false   D - false   E - false

1. ~A _____

2. ~C _____

3. A and B _____

4. A and C _____

5. B or C _____

6. B or D _____

7. C and E _____

8. C or E _____

9. A → B _____

10. B → C _____

11. C → E _____

12. E → D _____

13. (A and B) → D _____

14. (A and C) → E _____

Review of Notation and Propositions

Remember that a conditional statement is false only when the "if " part is true and the "then" part is false. In all other cases, the conditional statement is true.

➤ **A (true)   B (false)   A → B (false)**

Example

L = Lions are part of the cat family. (true)

M = Lions meow. (false)

L → M = If lions are part of the cat family, then lions meow. (false)

Tell whether these conditional statements are true or false. Write true or false on the line next to the logical notation for each part of the statement and for the entire if-then statement.

1. If 11 is an odd number, then 11 is not divisible by 2.

   O _____   ~D - <u>true</u>   O → ~D _____

2. If Germany is east of France, then Germany is east of England.

   EF _____   EE _____   EF → EE _____

3. If cats have fur, then dogs have feathers.

   CF _____   DF _____   CF → DF _____

4. If 33 is a multiple of 4, then 5 is a divisor of 41.

   TM _____   FD _____   TM → FD _____

5. If Earth is a planet, then Earth is not a star.

   P _____   ~S _____   P → ~S _____

6. If 6 is greater than 4 and 4 is greater than 2, then 6 is greater than 2.

   SF _____   FT _____   ST _____   (SF and FT) → ST _____

Introduction to Syllogisms

One of the oldest of all logic problems, the **syllogism**, was devised by the Greek philosopher Aristotle. It has three parts. The first two statements are called **premises**. The last statement is called the **conclusion**. The premises begin with the words "all," "some," or "no." The conclusion begins with the word, "therefore." Here is an example:

premise 1	*All bus drivers are patient.*
premise 2	*Mr. Butler is a bus driver.*
conclusion	*Therefore, Mr. Butler is patient.*

Syllogism Rules

- When both premises begin with "all," the conclusion must also use the word "all."
  All dogs are mammals.
  All mammals are warm blooded.
  Therefore, all dogs are warm blooded.

- When one premise begins with "no," "none" or "nothing," the conclusion must also contain these words.
  All dogs are mammals.
  No mammals lay eggs.
  Therefore, no dogs lay eggs.

- When one premise begins with "some," the conclusion must also use the word "some."
  Some dogs are small.
  All small things are cuddly.
  Therefore, some dogs are cuddly.

- If a premise does not contain the words "all," "some," "no," or "none," it is assumed that the statement begins with the word "all".
  All dogs have four legs.
  Things with four legs can run fast. (All things with four legs can run fast.)
  Therefore, all dogs can run fast.

- If the premise cites a singular case (refers to one thing or one person), the conclusion can only make a statement about that one person or thing — not about "all" things or "some" things.
  All dogs bark.
  Scuffy is a dog.
  Therefore, Scuffy barks.

- Conclusions that say "No _____ are _____" can be reversed.
  No dogs are fish can be written as *No fish are dogs.*

© Taylor & Francis Group · *MATH-A-LOGIC*   DOI: 10.4324/9781003236566-7

Analyzing Syllogisms

There are three sets of information in a syllogism. Each of the three statements must contain two of the three sets of information and each set must be used only twice. In one of the following examples the sets of information are *kittens, cute* and *Cuddles*. In the other syllogism, the sets are *beans, vegetables* and *healthy*.

Examples

All <u>kittens</u> are <u>cute</u>.
<u>Cuddles</u> is a <u>kitten</u>.
Therefore, <u>Cuddles</u> is <u>cute</u>.

All <u>beans</u> are <u>vegetables</u>.
All <u>vegetables</u> are <u>healthy</u>.
Therefore, all <u>beans</u> are <u>healthy</u>.

Underline the three sets of information in the following syllogisms. Use a different color for each set.

1. All multiples of 10 are multiples of 5.
   All multiples of 5 are divisible by 5.
   Therefore, all multiples of 10 are divisible by 5.

2. All ducks swim.
   All things that swim eat plants.
   Therefore, all duck eat plants.

3. All basketball players are tall.
   Bill is a basketball player.
   Therefore, Bill is tall.

4. All boys are males.
   Some males like cars.
   Therefore, some boys like cars.

5. All games are fun.
   Charades is a game.
   Therefore, charades is fun.

6. All fish live in the water.
   Some fish are predators.
   Therefore, some predators live in the water.

7. Write a syllogism that contains three different sets of information.

   _____

   _____

   _____

Validity

A syllogism can be either valid or invalid depending on whether the conclusion is supported by the premises. It doesn't matter whether the premises themselves are true or false. To be valid, the conclusion must follow logically from the premises.

Examples

All girls are females.
Some girls wear ponytails.
Therefore, all females wear ponytails.
invalid

All flowers have leaves.
All violets are flowers.
Therefore, all violets have leaves.
valid

Decide if these syllogisms are valid or invalid. Remember to check to see that each of the three sets of information is repeated twice.

1. All parallelograms have four sides.
   All figures with four sides are quadrilaterals.
   Therefore, all parallelograms are quadrilaterals.   valid   invalid

2. X is an even number.
   All even numbers are divisible by 2.
   Therefore, X is divisible by 2.   valid   invalid

3. All students go to school.
   All people who go to school are smart.
   Therefore, all smart people go to school.   valid   invalid

4. All birds have wings.
   All things with wings can fly.
   Therefore, all birds can fly.   valid   invalid

5. All pigs are pink.
   Porky is pink.
   Therefore, Porky is a pig.   valid   invalid

6. All oceans contain fish.
   All oceans contain whales.
   Therefore, all whales are fish.   valid   invalid

Crafting Conclusions

Write a valid conclusion for each of the following syllogisms.

1. All vegetables are healthy.
   Carrots are vegetables.

   Therefore, _____

2. All rabbits are mammals.
   No mammals can fly.

   Therefore, _____

3. Some countries have armies.
   All armies have weapons.

   Therefore, _____

4. All oaks are trees.
   All trees have roots.

   Therefore, _____

5. All squares have 4 sides.
   No figures with 4 sides are pentagons.

   Therefore, _____

6. All decimals can be written as fractions.
   .75 is a decimal.

   Therefore, _____

7. Some triangles are right triangles.
   All right triangles have a 90° angle.

   Therefore, _____

8. All factors of 6 are factors of 12.
   All factors of 12 are factors of 24.

   Therefore, _____

Sizing Up Syllogisms

Remember that a conclusion that follows logically from its two premises is valid. If the two premises do not support the conclusion, the syllogism is invalid. It doesn't matter if the premises are true or not.

Examples

All dancers are graceful.
Butch is graceful.
Therefore, Butch is a dancer.
invalid

All flowers are pretty.
A daisy is a flower.
Therefore, a daisy is pretty.
valid

Read the following syllogisms and tell whether they are valid or invalid.

1. All students are smart.
   Julie is a student.
   Therefore, Julie is smart.
   valid   invalid

2. All multiples of 10 are even.
   No even numbers are odd.
   Therefore, no multiples of 10 are odd.
   valid   invalid

3. All chocolate things are yummy.
   All peppermint things are yummy.
   Therefore, all chocolates are peppermints.
   valid   invalid

4. All birds lay eggs.
   All sparrows are birds.
   Therefore, all sparrows lay eggs.
   valid   invalid

5. Some spiders are poisonous.
   All poisonous things are dangerous.
   Therefore, some spiders are dangerous.
   valid   invalid

6. All circles are round.
   No round things are square.
   Therefore, no circles are square.
   valid   invalid

7. No squares are triangles.
   All triangles have three sides.
   Therefore, some squares have three sides.
   valid   invalid

8. All weight lifters are strong.
   Elsie is strong.
   Therefore, Elsie is a weight lifter.
   valid   invalid

© Taylor & Francis Group · *MATH-A-LOGIC*

Syllogism Practice

Write a valid conclusion for each syllogism.

1. All acute angles are less than 90°.
   Angle ABC is an acute angle.

   Therefore, _____

2. No multiples of 4 are odd.
   16 is a multiple of 4.

   Therefore, _____

3. Prime numbers have no divisors other than 1 and the number.
   17 is prime.

   Therefore, _____

4. All odd numbers can be expressed as 2n + 1.
   27 is an odd number.

   Therefore, _____

5. All islands are surrounded by water.
   Hawaii is an island.

   Therefore, _____

6. Some novels are adventure stories.
   All adventure stories are interesting.

   Therefore, _____

7. Some triangles are equiangular.
   All equiangular triangles are equilateral.

   Therefore, _____

Syllogism Review

Tell whether these syllogisms are valid or not. Circle the correct answer.

1. Some cars are Toyotas.
   All Toyotas are manufactured by a Japanese company.
   Therefore, all cars are manufactured by a Japanese company.
   valid   invalid

2. All left-handed people are creative.
   Joe is left-handed.
   Therefore, Joe is creative.
   valid   invalid

3. All sweaters are knit.
   All knit things are made of yarn.
   Therefore, all knit things are sweaters.
   valid   invalid

Write a valid conclusion for the following.

4. All trout are fish.
   All fish are cold-blooded.

   Therefore, _____

5. Some shoes are sports shoes.
   All sports shoes are sturdy.

   Therefore, _____

6. All suns are stars.
   No stars are planets.

   Therefore, _____

7. All continents are large.
   Africa is a continent.

   Therefore, _____

Use logical thinking to solve these problems.

1. Hilary has 10 pets that are cats, dogs and birds. She has twice as many cats as dogs. Together her pets have a total of 38 legs. How many of each kind of pet does she have?

2. Every 2 people share a jump rope and every 3 people share a ball. The teacher has just enough equipment so that all students can play with a ball at the same time and later in the class they can all jump rope at the same time. How many people are in the class if the total number of balls and jump ropes used during P.E. is 25?

3. During art class every 2 people share finger paints. Every 3 people share paste, and every 4 people share a water jar. How many people are in the art class if there are a total of 39 jars of paint, paste and water on the desks at the beginning of class?

Use logical thinking to solve these problems.

1. Hank collects baseball cards. He has twice as many pitchers as catchers. He has three times as many base players as catchers. He has one more outfielder than the number of catchers. He has a total of 50 cards. How many pitchers, catchers, outfielders, and basemen does he have?

2. Jed owns many forms of transportation — cars, bikes, motorcycles, and skateboards. He has a total of 8 vehicles with a total of 24 wheels. How many 4-wheel and 2-wheel vehicles does he have? If he has three times as many skateboards as cars, and the number of cars equals the number of motorcycles; how many does he have of each kind of vehicle?

3. Room 6 is having a pizza party. They want to have plenty of pizzas for everyone so they order one sausage pizza for every 2 people, one pepperoni for every 3 people, and one vegetarian for every 4 people. If 65 pizzas are ordered, how many people will be at the party?

Use logical thinking to solve these problems.

1. When Diedra lines up her stuffed animals she has three times as many mammals as birds and reptiles together. She has twice as many birds as reptiles. Her total collection is 24 animals. How many are birds, reptiles and mammals?

2. Doug is arranging for games for Game Night. He is planning on 1 Scrabble for every 4 people, 1 Clue for every 6 people, 1 checkers for every 2 people, and one ping pong for every 4 people. There will be 32 people at Game Night. How many of each game will he have to have available so all people can play a game at the same time?

3. Jamie exercises by running. He runs 3 kilometers on Monday, Wednesday and Friday, 4 kilometers on Tuesday and Thursday, 5 kilometers on Saturday, and 1 kilometer on Sunday. If he clocked a total of 15 kilometers for the week and he ran five days during the week, on which days did he run?

Use logical thinking to solve these problems.

1. Mrs. Krimshaw doesn't have enough
   books for everyone in her class. Every 2
   people share a health book, and every 4
   people share a music book. She does,
   however, have a science book for every
   person. If she has a total of 42 health,
   music and science books, how many
   students does she have?

2. Three generations of Dawsons gathered for a family
   dinner. There were 4 females and 3 males, 2
   grandparents, 2 grandchildren, 3 daughters, 1 son, 1
   uncle, 2 mothers, 2 fathers, and 1 son-in-law. What is
   the relationship of each of the 7 people gathered at the
   table?

3. Ted holds 8 coins (quarters, nickels, and dimes) in his
   hand. He has the same number of quarters as dimes.
   Altogether he has $1.15. What coins does he have?

Use logical thinking to solve these problems.

1. The members of the pep squad arrived at the game in two cars. When the first car arrived, there were three times as many girls as boys. When the second car arrived, the total squad had twice as many girls as boys. How were the 9 squad members divided between the two cars?

2. Katie and Bryce have written 12 books between the two of them. Katie has written twice as many books as Bryce. They wrote the same number of mysteries, but Katie wrote three times as many adventure stories as Bryce and three times as many comedies as him. When their books are added together, the number of mysteries equals the number of adventure stories which equals the number of comedies. How many of each kind of story did each person write?

3. The number of students in grades 4, 5 and 6 is 96. The 4th and 5th grades have 60 students. The 5th and 6th grades have 64 students. The 4th and 6th grades have 68 students. How many are in each grade?

Use logical thinking to solve these problems.

1. John has four puppies named Mutt, Miff, Biff and Buff. When he weighs Mutt and Miff, the total weight of the two puppies is 10 pounds. When he weighs Biff and Buff, the total weight of the two dogs is 13 pounds. When he weighs Mutt and Buff, the total weight is 14 pounds. How much will Miff and Biff weigh if they are put on the scale together?

2. What five weights could you choose so that using one or more of the weights, you can make any weight between 1 kilogram and 25 kilograms?

3. How can you string these nine beads on a string in such a way that similar shapes are not touching and similar patterns are not touching (for example, two stripes cannot be next to each other and 2 circles cannot be next to each other)?

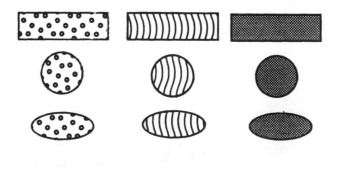

Use logical thinking to solve these problems.

1. Hilarie practices piano half as long as she practices tennis. She does homework for an hour more than she practices tennis and 2 hours more than she watches television. She spends half an hour eating dinner, which is half the amount of time she spends watching television. How much time does she spend on each activity every night?

2. Fill in the calendar in such a way that the sum of the numbers in box A is 44 and the sum of the numbers in box B is 84.

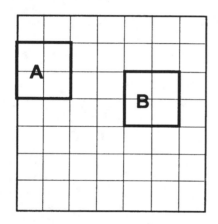

3. Here are three views of the same cube.

What symbol is opposite each side?

Use logical thinking to solve these problems.

1. George feeds his rabbits lettuce, carrots and rabbit chow. He feeds them twice as much carrots as lettuce and three times as much chow as carrots. Last week he fed them 27 pounds of food. How much of each kind of food did he buy?

2. Use the following clues to decipher the symbols for the numbers 0 through 9.

a. ♦ x ♦ = ☒ ☺   b. ■ x ■ = ✿ ♦

c. ✿ x ♦ = ♦ ●   d. ♦ + ☺ = ☺ ★

e. ☒ - ○ = ♦   f. ○ + ○ = ☺ ★

g. ■ + ● = ☺ ♦   h. ☉ x ☉ = ✿

i. ★ + ☉ = ☉   j. ○ x ♦ = ☺ ○

☺ = _____   ✿ = _____

■ = _7_   ♦ = _____

☉ = _____   ★ = _____

♦ = _____   ● = _____

☒ = _____   ○ = _____

3. Lil is serving drinks to a large group at the restaurant. She brings milk and soda to 5 people. Nine people order water only. Three people order soda and water. Four people drink water and milk. Fourteen drink only milk. Thirteen drink only soda. She brings all three drinks to only 2 people. How many milks does she bring? How many sodas does she bring? How many waters does she bring?

Answers

Lesson 1, pg. 4
1. 19
2. 28
3. 17
4. 65
5. 37
6. 1/12
7. 33
8. 29
9. 70
10. 11/20
11. 7/50
12. 6 5/6
13. 56
14. 18
15. ⊞

Lesson 2, pg. 5
1. 9
2. 31
3. 13
4. 50
5. 60
6. 17
7. 21
8. 14
9. 10 10/20
10. 6/10
11. 11.2
12. .25
13. 43
14. 10.5
15. 21

Lesson 3, pg. 6
1. 32
2. 81
3. 1/64
4. .001
5. 80
6. 32/243
7. 70,707
8. 16/6250
9. .003125
10. 8.1
11. 360
12. 50
13. 130
14. 1/108
15. 432

Lesson 4, pg. 7
1. 15, 6
2. 19, 13
3. 13, 21
4. 45, 40
5. 162, 3
6. 5, 4/5
7. 81, 27/81
8. 1/19, 1/23
9. .8, .08
10. 26, 42
11. 32, 2
12. 5, 45
13. 54, 108
14. 1.11, 2.11
15. 2, 32

Lesson 5, pg. 8
1. 21, 27
2. 50, 61
3. .375, .1875
4. 96, 6
5. 53, 86
6. 6,060.6, 60,606
7. 6/6, 7/6
8. 6, 46
9. 11 1/16, 12
10. 7776, 46,656
11. 30, 5
12. 36, 42
13. 62, 124
14. 156, 216
15. 26, 33
16. 3, 10

Lesson 6, pg. 9
1. 978, 9780
2. 56, 72
3. 2.5, .25
4. 456, 567
5. 22, 29
6. 9, 5
7. 1/3, 1/16
8. 12/21, 14/23
9. .900196, .0900196
10. 6, 5
11. 13, 11
12. 36, 49
13. .20, .30
14. 1/6, 1/7
15. 13/18, 15/21
16. 3, 6

Lessons 7, pg. 10
1. 1 cube - 5   2 cubes - 9   3 cubes -13   10 cubes - 41
2. 870 cm.
3. 10, 55

Lesson 8, pg. 11
1. 3, 6, 105
2. 12,345,654,321
3. 75 kg.

Lesson 9, pg. 12
1. 1 11 55 165 330
2. $(x - 2) \cdot 180$, 1800°
3. $6, $20, $380

Lesson 10, pg. 13
1. 32 plants
2. 31, 93, 3100
3. $15.00

Lesson 11, pg. 14
1. b
2. d
3. h
4. g
5. f
6. c
7. e
8. a

Lesson 12, pg. 15
1. 7
2. 90
3. 5/10
4. 761
5. 42
6. 9
7. 8
8. 130
9. 81
10. 16
11. 78
12. 5

Lesson 13, pg. 16
1. b
2. b
3. c
4. a
5. a
6. c
7. b
8. a
9. c

Lesson 14, pg. 17
1. 13/14
2. 25/144
3. 50
4. 15
5. 8/50
6. X
7. 18
8. 14
9. 6
10. 15
11. 24
12. 842

Lesson 15, pg. 18
1. 789
2. 432
3. $1.00
4. 75
5. 50
6. 1/8
7. 43
8. .25
9. 64
10. 1.25
11. 121
12. .40

Lesson 16, pg. 19
1. 101
2. 95
3. 33
4. 10
5. 12
6. 25
7. 31
8. 7.7
9. 31
10. 1.4
11. 9.3
12. 273

Lesson 17, pg. 20
Math Scores
Julia - 80   Josh - 96   Becca - 100
Ian - 78   Romeo - 98

Fast Animals
swift - 107   cheetah - 70
antelope - 60   man - 27
turtle - 21

Lesson 18, pg. 21
First Day of School
Tanya - 1st grade , room 5   Haley - 6th grade, room 2
Jonathan - 4th grade, room 17

Raffle Winners
1st - 471   3rd - 978
2nd - 156   4th - 327

Lesson 19, pg. 22
Family Ages
Amy - 4   Anton - 5   Alex - 10
Andy - 15   Mrs. Mendez - 34   Mr. Mendez - 33

Team Scores
Tigers - 94   Cubs - 79
Lions - 99   Eagles - 84

Lesson 20, pg. 23

Jim's Garden

1 sunflowers	2 sweet peas
3 squash	4 cabbage
5 tomatoes	6 peppers

Cake Lottery

Matt - 5	Charles - 23	Dee - 25
Catherine - 7	Stacy - 18	

Lesson 21, pg. 24

Animal Temperatures

peewee - 112°	goat - 104°	anteater – 74°
lizard - 98°	frog - 80°	icefish - 30°

Space Jumper

Jupiter - .41 meters, 16	Neptune - .82 meters, 2
Saturn - .85 meters, 19	Venus - 1.11 meters, 0
Mars - 2.60 meters, 2	Mercury - 2.68 meters, 0

Lesson 22, pg. 25

1. 47	2. 69	3. 26
4. 50	5. 37	

Lesson 23, pg. 26

1. 137	2. 717	3. 541	4. 789

Lesson 24, pg. 27

1. 9, 5	2. 25, 10	3. 8, 6
4. 10, 4	5. 23, 19	6. 4, 2
7. 15, 3	8. 12, 3	9. 15, 10
10. 17, 1	11. 6, 3	12. 7, 2

Lesson 25, pg. 28

1. 15, 16	2. 2, 17	3. 3, 5
4. 37, 4	5. 21, 3	6. 60, 4
7. 14, 3	8. 52, 14	9. 16, 4
10. 45, 9	11. 23, 32	12. 5, 11

Lesson 26, pg. 29

1.
```
  75
 -25
  50
```
2.
```
  12
 +10
  22
```
3.
```
  43
 -29
  14
```
4.
```
 497
- 72
 425
```
5.
```
  99
 +44
 143
```
6.
```
  44
 +17
  61
```
7.
```
  26
 +36
  62
```
8.
```
  98
 - 14
  84
```
9.
```
 123
+318
 441
```
10.
```
 567
+ 89
 656
```
11.
```
  48
+  86
 134
```

Lesson 27, pg. 30

1.
```
 333
 x 4
1332
```
2.
```
 15
x 5
 75
```
3.
```
 28
x 2
 56
```
4.
```
 84
x 5
420
```
5.
```
 77
x 3
231
```
6.
```
123
x 4
492
```
7. 6$\overline{)366}$ → 61

8. 7$\overline{)574}$ → 82

9. 10$\overline{)1010}$ → 101

10. 16$\overline{)6416}$ → 401

11. 9$\overline{)261}$ → 29

Lesson 28, pg. 31

One possible arrangement is given. Other arrangements are possible.

1.
```
10 20 30
   15
   25
```
4.
```
7 9 1
  3
```
2.
```
6 8 10
   7
   9
```
5.
```
   12
6 10 14
   8
```
3.
```
13 15 17
   11
   19
```
6.
```
   5
 6 7 8
   9
```

Lesson 29, pg. 32

One possible arrangement is given. Other arrangements are possible.

1.
```
    2
    4
1 3 5 7 9
    6
    8
```
2.
```
       6
      12
3 9 15 21 27
      18
      24
```
3.
```
2 6 10
  8
  4
```
4.
```
      11
      13
10 12 14 16 18
      15
      17
```
5.
```
6 8 9 10 12
    13
    7
    11
    5
```
6.
```
       16
        8
4 12 20 28 36
       24
       32
```

Lesson 30, pg. 33

One possible arrangement is given for each problem. Other arrangements are possible.

1.
```
2 7 6
9 5 1
4 3 8
```
2.
```
12 14 4
 2 10 18
16  6  8
```

78

Lesson 30, continued

3.   18 21 6   4.   9 10 5
     3 15 27   4 8 12
   24 9 12   11 6 7

5.   16 12 32   6. 40 15 20
   36 20 4   5 25 45
    8 28 24   30 35 10

Lesson 31, pg. 34

One possible arrangement is given. Other arrangements are possible.

1.   26 24 34   2. 10 5 6
   36 28 20   3 7 11
   22 32 30   8 9 4

3.   39 29 31   4. 13 12 17
   25 33 41   18 14 10
   35 37 27   11 16 15

5.   11 12 7   6. 14 10 30
    6 10 14   34 18 2
   10 8 9   6 26 22

Lesson 32, pg. 35

1. divide by 2; 10, 9
2. subtract 6; 86, 75
3. inverse; 23/10, 5/19
4. add 1/2; 1
5. divide by 10; 180, 5.08
6. mult. by 10, add 5; 115, 265
7. subtract 15; 30, 78
8. divide by 3; 14, 31
9. square root; 6, 12
10. add 101; 164, 145
11. multiply by the next consecutive number; 182
12. divide by 5; 3, 19

Lesson 33, pg. 36

1. multiply by 2; 20, 32
2. divide by 3; 100, 2
3. mult. inverse; 1/7, 1/32
4. add 3; 19, 25
5. subtract 10; 40, 36
6. square root; 10, 5
7. multiply by 2; 2/5, 8/9
8. multiply by 3, add 3; 66
9. x−1/x; 26/27, 4
10. square; 64, 196
11. add 12; 31, 52
12. subtract 11; 22, 17

Lesson 34, pg. 37

1. d   2. e   3. f   4. c
5. g   6. b   7. a   8. g
9. h   10. {red, orange, yellow, green, blue, purple}
11. {3, 6, 9, 12, 15, 18}   12. {2, 4, 6, 8, 10}
13. answers will vary

Lesson 35, pg. 38

1. {1, 2, 3, 4, 5, 6, 7, 8, 9}
2. {2, 4, 6...98}
3. answers will vary
4. {March, May}
5. {10, 20, 30, ... 90}
6. {1/5, 2/5, 3/5...}
7. {1, 3, 5, 7...}
8. answers will vary
9. answers will vary
10. {1, 2, 3, 6}
11. {tops, stop, pots, spot, post}
12. {10, 11, 12...199}

Lesson 36, pg. 39

1. B   2. F   3. K
5. D   6. C   7. H   8. A
9. E   10. G   11. J   12. 5-D, 7-H

Lesson 37, pg. 40

answers will vary

Lesson 38, pg. 41

1. {cat, dog, fish, turtle}   2. {1, 2, 3, 4, 5, 6, 7, 8}
3. {boys and girls in room 4}   4. {1, 2, 3, 4, ...}
5. {1, 2, 3, 4, 6, 8, 12}   6. {1, a, 2, b, 3, c, 4, d, 5, e, 6}
7. {p, a, i, n, t, b, r, u, s, h}   8. {s, p, r, i, t, e, c, o, k}
9. {m, o, n, d, a, y, t, u, e, s} 10. {0, 1/2, 1, 11/2, 2}

Lesson 39, pg. 42

1. {10, 20}   2. {2, 4, 8, 16}   3. {1, 2, 3, 6 }
4. {l, y}   5. { s}   6. {h, a, i}
7. {e}   8. {d, a, y}   9. {f, i, s}

Lesson 40, pg. 43

1. {cat, dog, fish, bird, frog, lizard}, {fish}
2. {pie, cake, peas, carrots}, { }
3. {January, February, December}, {January, February}
4. {h, o, m, e, l, y, i, d, u, s}, {h, o, e}
5. {l, i, o, n, t, i, g, e, r}, {i}
6. {2, 4, 6, 8, 10, 12, 16, 20}, {4, 8, 12}
7. {boys and girls in the 4th grade}, { }
8. {o, r, a, n, g, e, v, i, l, t}, {o, e}

Lesson 41, pg. 44

1. {p, e, a, r, o, n, g}
   {a, e, r}   {a, r, e, g, p}
2. {1, 2, 3, 4, 5, 6, 8, 10, 12}
   {2, 4, 6, 8, 12}   {2, 4, 6, 8, 10}
3. {a, y}
   {g, e, r, m, a, n, y, h, u, i, t, l} {r, a, n, y, i, t, l, g}
4. {1, 2, 3, 4, 5, 6, 9, 10, 12, 18}
   {1, 2}   {1, 2, 3, 4, 6, 12}

Lesson 42, pg. 45

1. c   2. a   3. b

Lesson 43, pg. 46

1. 1   2. 3   3. 4   4. 2
5. 2   6. 1   7. 5   8. 2
9. 1   10. 4   11. 4   12. 7
13. 1   14. 3   15. 4   16. 2   17. 5

Lesson 44, pg. 47

Lesson 45, pg. 48

1.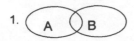

2.

3.

4.

5.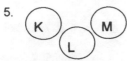

6.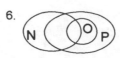

Lesson 46, pg. 49

Answers will vary but should show the information in the intersecting circles.

Lesson 47, pg. 50

1. 6 jumpers, $238.00
2. cake and ice cream - 10   ice cream and/or cake - 18
   cake - 13   ice cream - 15

Lesson 48, pg. 51

1. 14 cats   17 dogs   6 bids
2. art - 28   computer - 31   photography - 25

Lesson 49, pg. 52

1. flowers - 32   herbs - 14   vegetables - 23
2. baseball - 24   soccer - 19   players - 77

Lesson 50, pg. 53

1. f	2. i	3. c	4. a
5. j	6. d	7. h	8. b
9. e	10. g		

Lesson 51, pg. 54

1. a	2. f	3. c	4. h
5. b	6. e	7. d	8. g

9. NP and O   10. FP → FS   11. EV → YH

Lesson 52, pg. 55

1. BC → JT   2. YP → CO   3. CO → MM
4. WP → D   5. MP → CC   6. WF → TS
7. TW → TE   8. TE → F
9. YP → MM, If you keep pouring, then it will make a mess.
   TW → F - If a number is divisible by 20, then it is divisible by 5.

Lesson 53, pg. 56

1. The triangle does not have three sides (~TS)
2. It is raining. (R)
3. The square is not a quadrilateral. (~SQ)
4. The sum is not even and the sum is not odd.
   (~ SE and ~ SO)
5. Mother cannot go or Father can go. (~ MG or FG)
6. The cat is not cute or the dog is not dirty. (~CC or ~DD)
7. It is not raining and it is snowing. (~R and S)

Lesson 54, pg. 57

1. a) T	b) T	c) T
d) T	e) F	
2. a) T	b) F	c) F
d) T	e) F	
3. a) F	b) T	c) F
d) T	e) F	
4. a) T	b) T	c) T
d) T	e) T	

Lesson 55, pg. 58

1. T - A triangle does not have three sides. (~TA)
2. T - B is not a better grade than D. (~BB)
3. F - The product of two even numbers is an even number. (PE)
4. T - The sun is not a star and the sun is not a planet. (~SS and ~SP)
5. F - Cats cannot fly or birds cannot swim. (~CF or ~BS)
6. T - Twelve is not even or forty-three is not odd. (~TE or ~FO)
7. T - A rectangle is not a quadrilateral. (~RQ)
8. T - The hypotenuse is not the longest side of a triangle. (~ HL)
9. T - Twelve does not have six factors or twelve is not even. (~SF or ~E)

Lesson 56, pg. 59

1. T, T, T	2. T, T, T	3. F, F, T
4. T, T, T	5. F, T, T	6. T, F, F
7. T, T, T	8. T, F, F	

Lesson 57, pg. 60

1. F	2. T	3. T	4. F
5. T	6. T	7. F	8. F
9. T	10. F	11. T	12. T
13. F	14. T		

Lesson 58, pg. 61

1. T, T, T	2. T, T, T	3. T, F, F
4. F, F, T	5. T, T, T	6. T, T, T, T

Lesson 60, pg. 62

1. multiples of 10, multiples of 5, divisible by 5
2. ducks, things that swim, eat plants
3. basketball players, tall, Bill
4. boys, males, like cars
5. games, fun, charades
6. fish, live in the water, predators
7. answers will vary

Lesson 61, pg. 64

1. valid	2. valid	3. invalid
4. valid	5. invalid	6. invalid

Lesson 62, pg. 65

1. carrots are healthy.   2. no rabbits can fly.
3. some countries have weapons.
4. all oaks have roots.   5. no squares are pentagons.
6. .75 can be written as a fraction.
7. some triangles have a 90° angle.
8. all factors of 6 are factors of 24.

Lesson 63, pg. 66

1. valid   2. valid   3. invalid   4. valid
5. valid   6. valid   7. invalid   8. invalid

Lesson 64, pg. 67

1. angle ABC is less than 90°.
2. 16 is not odd.
3. 17 has only 1 and 17 as divisors.
4. 27 can be expressed as 2n + 1.
5. Hawaii is surrounded by water.
6. some novels are interesting.
7. some triangles are equilateral.

Lesson 65, pg. 68

1. invalid   2. valid   3. invalid
4. all trout are cold-blooded.   5. some shoes are sturdy.
6. no suns are planets.   7. Africa is large.

Lesson 66, pg. 69

1. 3 dogs, 6 cats, 1 bird   2. 30 people
3. 36 people

Lesson 67, pg. 70

1. 14 pitchers, 7 catchers, 8 outfielders, 21 basemen
2. 1 car, 1 motorcycle, 3 bicycles, 3 skateboards; 4 two-wheel
   vehicles, 4 four-wheel vehicles
3. 60 people

Lesson 68, pg. 71

1. 2 reptiles, 4 birds, 18 mammals
2. Many combinations are possible. The simplest is to have
   two of every game.
3. Mon., Wed., Fri., Sat., Sun. or
   Mon., Tues., Wed., Thurs., Sun. or
   Tues., Wed., Thurs., Fri., Sun.

Lesson 69, pg. 72

1. 24 students
2. 1 grandmother, 1 grandfather, 1 mother (daughter), 1
   father (son-in-law), 1 uncle (son) 2 grandchildren
   (daughters)
3. 3 quarters, 3 dimes, 2 nickels

Lesson 70, pg. 73

1. car 1 - 3 girls, 1 boy   car 2 - 2 boys, 3 girls
2. Katie - 2 mysteries, 3 adventure, 3 comedies
   Bryce - 2 mysteries, 1 adventure, 1 comedy
3. 4th grade - 32 students   5th grade - 28 students
   6th grade - 36 students

Lesson 71, pg. 74

1. 9 pounds
2. 1, 2, 4, 8, 10 kilograms
3. several arrangements are possible. One arrangement is as
   follows:

Lesson 72, pg.75

1. piano - 1 hour   tennis - 2 hours
   homework - 3 hours   television - 1 hour
   eating - 1/2 hour
2.   0 1 2 3 4 5 6
      7 8 9 10 11 12 13
     14 15 16 17 18 19 20
     21 22 23 24 25 26 27
     28 29 30
3. ●   opposite ☼   ■ opposite ☺
   ⌘ opposite ◆

Lesson 73, pg. 76

1. 3 pounds lettuce, 6 pounds carrots, 18 pounds chow
2. 0 = ★   4 = ☼   8 = ⊠
   1 = ☺   5 = ○   9 = ◆
   2 = ◉   6 = ●
   3 = ◢   7 = ■
3. milk - 25   soda - 23   water - 18